I AM NECESSARY

SO WORTH IT

By Jacqueline E. Russell

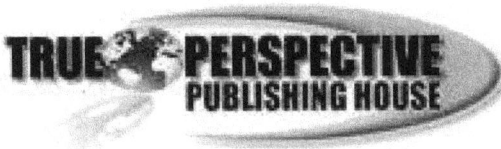

TRUE PERSPECTIVE PUBLISHING HOUSE

Acknowledgments

"For I know the plans I have for you," declares the LORD, "plans to prosper you and not to harm you, plans to give you hope and a future."

Jeremiah 29:11

I am eternally thankful to God for all that he has done in my life. For it is a constant reminder that without him I am nothing.

To the man that God prepared for me and me for him my husband. Thanks A.J. Russell for inspiring me to write and keep writing. You are the epitome of what each woman desires to have as a mate in their life. Your love, meekness, and pure heart makes my heart smile every day. I love you!

A very special thanks to my daughter Keninna Graham, who has always inspired me to want to do and be the very best me I possibly could. The love that I have for you has strengthened me in ways that I could never believe were possible.

To Mildred Spikes, my mom, thank you for teaching me to be a diligent worker. You always taught me to work for what I wanted and to be steadfast in doing so. I am so thankful that even in those times that you had to work and couldn't take us to church; you always had someone that would step in and fulfill that role in your absence.

To Jackie Belcher, my Dad, thanks for loving me unconditionally, and being supportive of me and my dreams.

To all my siblings, thank you for all the fights and disagreements we've had growing up as it made us have a bond that is inseparable. I love every one of you with the purest love. I continue to pray God's blessing upon you.

Thanks to my church families TWOL (The Way of Life, Ministries) and FMBC (First Missionary Baptist Church) for being supportive in all my endeavors. I love you all so much.

A heartfelt thank you to Stacey Dority for lending her words of transparency, strength, and encouragement on this piece of work!

Finally, thank you to True Perspective Publishing House, Sean Cort for believing in me and allowing me to make yet another part of my assignment a reality.

I would also like to express my gratitude to all of those that supported me in all my endeavors throughout this journey thus far. I am forever grateful to you!

Introduction

Joslyn is newly married to Andy James Richardson. She and her daughter Jayla finally have the husband and father that they've longed for in their lives. Joslyn's practice, "J.J. Family Counseling", is doing quite well thanks to her previous client Elaine. After counseling Elaine and Dexter more than a year ago, Elaine is still promoting Joslyn's practice. Abigail Weekly, Darcie Green, Ramona Perez and Xanthia Curtly are four new clients and each of them has a unique situation going on in their lives and is seeking counsel from Joslyn to help sort out their issues. However, Joslyn is faced with an issue of her own.

A Note to my Sisters

This book is dedicated to every woman who has experienced issues in their lives that are a direct result of their choices or circumstances out of their control. You are not your choices or your circumstances! You are necessary and so worth it, regardless of your choices and circumstances. Don't let life define you! God has already done that! You are fearfully and wonderfully made! So get up, knock off the doubt, pity, and shame, and walk in your God given Space!

FOREWORD

I AM NECESSARY – SO WORTH IT, is a compound, validating statement! It resonates to the heart that has been broken, the mind that is confused and it reaches across the dichotomy of gender and ethnicities.

This book informs the readers of their value regardless of past mistakes and or failures – YOU ARE NOT what you do, nor what you have done. Everything and everyone God created has good within (Genesis 2:31). However, some decisions you choose can be for better or worse. He and He alone has the power to work ALL things together for good that you might encounter on this journey called life, when you lovingly look to Him and trust Him as your Lord and Savior (Romans 8:28).

I AM NECESSARY – SO WORTH IT deals with real life, relatable situations that you experience in this fallen world: fear, frustration, rejection, the need to be accepted, anger, hurt, betrayal, unforgiveness, forgiveness, reconciliation, restoration and relationships to list a few. For healing and deliverance to occur, it is *necessary* you be open and honest with yourself.

This book is helpful in guiding you to take a step of faith and leave the results to God. It encourages you to seek help and especially professional help when life becomes overwhelming and burdensome.

Each chapter is filled with captivating mystery. How will this dilemma end? I was greatly impacted by the openness and vulnerability each case scenario conveyed.

You are *necessary* and this book is so *worth* reading. So, go ahead, grab a cup of hot coffee, cold glass of iced tea, lemonade or the beverage of your choice. Sit back and relax as Mrs. Jackie Russell, Author, takes you on an unforgettable journey of complexities of life – life happens!

> Dr. Jo Ann J. Jameson, Assistant Pastor
> The Way of Life Ministries, Inc.
> Orlando, Florida.

Table of Contents

I AM NECESSARY – SO WORTH IT

A New Beginning

The constant buzzing of the alarm clock was giving Joslyn a major headache. She was too groggy to reach over and turn it off; therefore, she gave AJ (short for Andy James) a nudge in his arm to do it. He was tired as well but didn't hesitate to reach over and turn it off. It had only been two days since Joslyn and AJ were married and he had to leave on a business trip.

The thought of him leaving gave Joslyn a feeling of separation anxiety, like that of a toddler being separated from her mom for the first time. Joslyn knew that AJ had to return to work but having that prior knowledge didn't make his leaving any easier. However, she knew it was best; not to mention the fact that she too had to get back to work.

Her client list was growing rapidly because of her former client Elaine's word of mouth advertising. Elaine and Dexter had renewed their wedding vows and were really enjoying their newfound marriage and relationship with God. As a result, Elaine recommended a list of her friends and their friends to Joslyn's practice to seek help for their broken lives. Although she told them about her and Dexter's experience with Prophetess Barbara Gaines and what it did to enhance their lives, she wanted them to seek help from Joslyn as well.

Joslyn entered her office building bright and early on Monday morning wearing her new 3 Karat, white gold, diamond wedding ring. Everyone in the office was ranting and raving about how gorgeous it was and how radiant she looked. Joslyn felt everything that they were describing. She knew her ring was gorgeous, she felt gorgeous and knew that her smile exuded pure radiance and happiness; but most of all, for the first time in her life, she felt loved. It was a feeling of being renewed. Although she still was in such awe about how her life had been transformed and how she had grown as a counselor, wife, and a woman of God, she knew that her life was certainly in a different place. Joslyn was ready to take on the world and help every woman who encountered any of her past experiences.

After all the ruckus in the front office subsided, Joslyn retreated to her office to begin what would be a long day of checking email and phone messages and responding to potential client concerns. Joslyn set her black Michael Kors bag and brief case on the chair adjacent to her desk and walked over and looked at the city's view through the window behind her desk. In February, the flower garden right outside her window always made things seem beautiful even if things weren't so beautiful in her life. The bio-colored pansies in white, pink, purple and yellow lined the sidewalk right outside the window and when the sun shined on them just right, it was the most illuminating site.

The light that disembogues from the flowers warmed her on the inside and always spoke, "Everything is going to be okay", just like that of the Spirit of the Lord once you adhere to him.

Joslyn stood their staring at the flowers for a moment reflecting on how good God had been to her. Even in her mess, He was still good to her. She must have had a pensive look on her face because her new secretary Margaret entered and asked if she was okay. Joslyn assured Margaret that she was fine and asked her "Why do you ask?" Margaret stated that she had been standing there for more than two minutes calling Joslyn's name. Joslyn apologized and asked if she could help her with something. Margaret informed her that she had several messages that she had taken because her voice mail was full, and potential clients are waiting for responses to their calls. Joslyn thanked Margaret, sat down and began to review the written and verbal messages that needed responding too.

Who is Abigail?

Joslyn pressed 5200 on her phone to retrieve the fifteen messages that filled her voicemail.. She listened intently to the first message where a woman appeared to be sobbing uncontrollably and Joslyn couldn't make out what she was saying. The dial tone took over as she abruptly hung up.. Joslyn pressed next call and the woman was on the phone again, but this time she did state that her name is Abigail.

After stating her name, she said, "I know you are wondering who Abigail is?" Then she says, "I'm glad you asked I am a friend of Elaine's and she gave me your number. She told me to call you because I am having some problems in my life and I need help sorting them out. I don't have much money, but I can pay you in installments if you are okay with that. I don't want to take any medication because I know that ya'll shrinks like to give people medicine any time they come and see ya'll. I am not crazy, so please don't look at me crazy when I come to your office and don't write nothing down that implies that I am. I just want help sorting out my complicated life. I don't want to go into details about what my complications are over the phone but" ….and then the phone cuts off because she runs out of time and couldn't finish the message.

Joslyn proceeds to the next message and it is Abigail continuing from where she left off. She says, "Before the call hung up, I was saying, I don't want to go into details about my complications in life over the phone, therefore, I need to have a meeting with you. Please call me back at 555-5655, again that's 555-5655 and my name is Abigail with no last name. I don't feel comfortable leaving my last name on a stranger's voice mail okay, so don't take that personal. Anyway, call me back soon okay." The phone called ended and Joslyn sat and wondered, who is Abigail? Although Abigail said that she received Joslyn's number from Elaine (which Joslyn loved because of the word of mouth advertising that she was doing), Joslyn was a bit disquieted by the request that Abigail left on her answering service. Joslyn decided to review the notes that she had taken while listening to Abigail's message.

It was customary for Joslyn to take notes while listening to messages because she wanted to make sure that she had all the facts when she returned a call to a potential client. Joslyn noted that her number is 555-5655, she doesn't have the money to pay and apparently she doesn't have any insurance because she didn't mention it. She doesn't want me to look at her crazy or imply that she is; she doesn't want medication, she doesn't feel comfortable leaving her last name with a stranger, she didn't want to discuss anything over the phone, and she wanted a call back soon. Joslyn looked at the list of requests that she had written down and wondered yet again, who is Abigail?

Joslyn decided to return Abigail's call before she retrieved any more message, as she had become intrigued with the woman's dialogue and demeanor in her messages. Joslyn picked up her phone while looking at the number she had written down and dialed 555-5655 and waited for someone to answer. On the third ring, a man answers, "Hello" and Joslyn asks to speak with Abigail. The gentleman on the phone wanted to know what it was in reference to. Joslyn wasn't at liberty to divulge any information regarding who she was because of the doctor and patient/client confidentiality clause. Even though technically Abigail wasn't a client yet, she didn't want to take that chance. Therefore, Joslyn told him it was in reference to a referral from a friend of hers named Elaine. The gentleman yelled for Abigail to pick up the phone and suddenly there was a busy signal. Joslyn waits a few minutes trying to decide if she should call back or leave this bizarre situation alone. While she was contemplating on calling back, her phone rings and an unknown number appears on the caller ID. Joslyn answers, "Hello" and Abigail apologizes for hanging up and said she is calling from her cell phone while walking around the block. Joslyn asked," What was happening" and she stated matter-of-factly, "I said that I didn't want to speak over the phone." "Well, would you be available to come in tomorrow around nine o'clock in the morning to discuss your issue?" says Joslyn. Abigail agreed and they hung up.

Joslyn was a bit thrown off by this Abigail person because she was acting a bit strange and Joslyn had never experienced a potential client that was so vague with what was happening in her life.

Early the next morning, the aroma of Hazelnut and Vanilla Bean Coffee engulfed the house brewing downstairs in the kitchen. Jayla had decided to fix her and Joslyn some scrambled egg whites and turkey bacon, along with a pot of Hazelnut and Vanilla Bean Coffee before leaving for school and work. Jayla had grown so much and was so helpful with chores and meals around the house. As they sat and had breakfast they would always talk about their agenda for the day and their challenges as well. Jayla was concerned with a geometry test that she had to take after lunch because some of the formulas were a bit confusing.

Joslyn always told her to do her best and always go with the first answer that enters her thoughts because something had to have triggered that memory. Joslyn did talk about her first day back at work and how she was unable to get through and/ or respond to all the messages that were left on her voicemail or the ones that Margaret had taken for her. Joslyn was excited about the increase in business, but she was dreading the conversation that she was anticipating with Abigail all at the same time.

After Joslyn dropped Jayla off to school, she drove quietly to work. This is usually the time when she could clear her head and have a quiet moment with God prior to entering the chaos of the office. Joslyn drove for nearly twenty minutes before noticing that she was about to miss her exit to the office. Upon arriving at the office, she noticed a fair skinned, medium build, well maintenance, long, black wavy haired, African American woman standing near a white Jaguar.

Joslyn wondered if this could be Abigail, but she digressed from that thought because there was no way that this woman and the woman that left the messages, who she had spoken to, could be one in the same. Joslyn gathered her things and proceeded to walk into the building. As she approached the white Jaguar where the unknown woman was standing, she stopped her and asked, "Are you Joslyn

Richardson? Joslyn responded with, "Who's asking?" She stated, "Are you her?" Again, Joslyn said, "Who's asking?" Finally, she said, "Abigail". "Yes, I am Joslyn Richardson." "You scheduled an appointment with me at nine, so why are you standing here in the parking lot at eight o'clock?" Joslyn asked. Abigail, sounding a bit annoyed says, "Well if you must know I had to leave early because of personal reasons and if it's okay, I would wait until nine to be seen." Joslyn agreed and told her that she would see her inside at nine.

Joslyn was getting everything prepared because nine was quickly approaching and Abigail, no doubt, was watching every second on the clock. Margaret enters Joslyn's office and tells her that Abigail was ready to be seen by her even though she still had more than ten minutes until nine o'clock. Joslyn agreed to see Abigail earlier and told Margaret to show her in. Joslyn got the preliminaries out of the way by asking her about insurance and payment.

After that was discussed, Joslyn says to Abigail, "So, what brings you in to see me?" Abigail began by asking, "Will what I say in here stay strictly confidential?" Joslyn assured her that it would. Abigail began telling Joslyn about her complicated life. Abigail says, "I have been married to Roy for nine years and although I love him a lot and he provides for me a great deal, I am no longer in love with him. I am in love with his twin brother Ron. Ron and I have been secretly seeing each other four of the nine years that I have been married to Roy and I don't know what to do. Growing up I never had a man love me, lavish me with gifts or simply take care of me.

All they ever did was use me for my body and dump me for the next woman. So, when Roy came along and pampered me and later asked me to marry him, I jumped for that opportunity because I had never experienced that kind of attention before. Then, I met his twin brother Ron on a family vacation. We hit it off immediately. He is 5'11'', with dark skin, pearly white teeth, a hard body, and he is very charismatic. He and Roy are twins and have a lot in common, but there are two things that are certainly different about them; First thing is, Roy doesn't pay attention to me, he just buys me things; and Ron inspires me to be a better me and Roy doesn't. Secondly, Roy is very controlling and doesn't want me to pursue anything in life. He believes that if I did anything on my own, it would count him out because I will become independent and not need him anymore.

His treating me this way has caused great stress and unhappiness in my life. I know that this thing with Ron is wrong, but it feels right. I also know that I should have waited and not married because I felt that someone had real interest in me for the first time in my life. I just felt like I would never be good enough to have a man like Roy and when he asked me to marry him, I did." Abigail stopped talking and just sat there with tears streaming down her face. Joslyn handed her a tissue and then asked the question

that she normally would ask at the intake of a potential

client. "Abigail, what do you plan to get out of your

sessions with me?" Joslyn always asked this question

because she wanted to be sure that the client really wanted

to be helped and that she would not be spinning her wheels

trying to sort through a client's issues if they weren't

certain that they wanted to do this. Abigail says, "I really

need your help because I don't like what I am doing

because I know it is not right; and I want to know why I did

this in the first place. I plan to finally come to grips with

who Abigail is!" Abigail's answer satisfied Joslyn and she

told her that she would indeed take her as a client.

She told her that she needed to stop by Margaret's

desk on her way out, because they were out of time for

their thirty-minute session and fill out the necessary

documents and schedule her next appointment a week from

today. Joslyn stood and walked her to the door and told her that she looked forward to working with her.

Joslyn sat down at her desk and reflected on what she was just told by Abigail and knew that she had her work cut out for her. Joslyn started reviewing the messages that Margaret had taken for her before retrieving those from her voice mail. As she was fumbling through the sticky notes, she came across a message that was a bit puzzling to her. The message read, "Call me when you get a chance, Deanna." Joslyn was puzzled by this message because Deanna was not someone she associated with anymore.

Deanna was an old friend of hers that she hadn't spoken too since it was said that she cheated with her ex-husband Tristan while they were married. Deanna would not admit that any of it was true when she was asked about it; however, after the divorce and Joslyn had moved on, Deanna admitted that she indeed had been with him. Joslyn couldn't understand for the life of her why Deanna would want to speak with her after all this time, but there was one

thing that she did know concerning Deanna, that she was

not someone to be trusted.

He's Rearing His Head

Joslyn had finished her last appointment and was going to start returning phone calls as soon as she walked her last client through the office and out to the foyer. After letting the client out because Margaret had to leave on an emergency, up walks Ms. Deanna wearing six-inch heels, a toddler skirt, a halter top with 26-inch, black, wavy Indian hair tousled over her head. Deanna was never much to be concerned with because she was no bigger than a buck- o -five, but her mouth was as large as the Atlantic Ocean and as loud as one hundred zebras' all roaring at the same time. Joslyn told the client that she would see her next week and told Deanna to follow her to her office. Joslyn was very curious about this visit because she hadn't returned her call, so what would make her just pop up to the office. Joslyn asked if she would like coffee, tea, or water and Deanna refused a drink. Joslyn wanted to get right to the point of this sudden visit because she knew that this would be something that the devil was using to rear his head.

Deanna started with small talk congratulating Joslyn on her marriage and saying that she was happy for her and all. Joslyn politely said, "Thanks" and asked "What did you really come here for Deanna? I know it wasn't for small talk, so what is it?" Deanna sighed and then said ,"I just wanted to tell you that Andy's family is spreading nasty rumors about you and that they are very upset that he married you and are saying negative things to him in an effort to get him to reconsider his marriage to you." Joslyn was appalled at what was coming out of Deanna's mouth. Joslyn knew that Deanna knew everyone in the neighborhood, but who would trust saying or telling

Deanna anything about anyone because they knew she

would go back and tell the other party. Joslyn just stood

there for a moment trying to gather her thoughts because it

came as such a shock to her. After a moment or two of

wondering how and why Deanna was saying this, she

asked, "Where did you get this information; and why are

you telling me this? We are not friends like that anymore!"

Deanna said, "I wanted you to know because his sister

Larissa was going around town asking everyone about your

past and she just happened to come to me and ask me."

Deanna went on to say, "Someone directed her to me

because they said that we were once good friends back in

the day, and I would be the one to give her the 411 about

you. I did tell her about you and Tristan, Baby and Gabe. I

didn't know first off why she wanted all the information

until I finished telling her and she said that "My brother

shouldn't have married her!" Deanna paused with a look of

distress on her face and then said, "I am sorry that I told her anything about you and I am sorry for what happened between me and Tristan all those years ago." Joslyn just stood there looking with a blank stare as if she had just witness a crime. Deanna stood silent as well until she pretended to start to cry like Joslyn didn't remember she could do that at the drop of a hat like they do in movie scenes when a love one is lost.

Joslyn stopped Deanna in her tracks with her drama and told her that she accepted her apology and that she was in a different place now. Joslyn thanked her for being kind enough to let her know what was going on through the rumor mill as she was out of the loop with that sort of thing since she had changed for the better with God in her life and all. Deanna apologized again! Joslyn accepted, thanked her again, and walked her out.

Joslyn went back to her office and sat there wondering "Okay Lord what is this about and why?"

Joslyn finished up her paperwork and headed home. While Joslyn was on her way home, her mind was all over the place. The questions went on and on. Joslyn wondered, "Why is his sister concerned about me and my past? What does my past have to do with his sister and why would she be telling him to reconsider his marriage to me?" Those questions were playing over and over in Joslyn's head when her phone rang, and it was AJ.

AJ was always jovial and loving, even more so when he was away on business and they spoke by phone. AJ knew right away that something was wrong because Joslyn was a bit quiet on the phone. Joslyn didn't hesitate to ask him about his family and most of all, his sister. AJ wasn't the kind of man that would sugar coat anything, nor was he the type to lie about anything. AJ told Joslyn that his family, especially his sister had a problem with him marrying her because she had heard about her relationship with Baby and felt that she wasn't, at best, of his caliber.

Joslyn couldn't believe what she was hearing. How could his sister pass judgment on a person that she doesn't know for herself?" Not to mention, "Why would anyone tell a grown man that he needed to reconsider his marriage that has nothing to do with them?" AJ also said that he told Larissa and the other family members that were concerned about him and his marriage that he knew about Joslyn's past and that God ordained his marriage and that's that! Joslyn became very annoyed with what had taken place. She had no idea that they felt this way, or the fact that they had already gone to AJ with it. Joslyn just listened as AJ continued to tell her that he told his family that they would respect her regardless of the issues that they had with the situation. The more Joslyn listened to him explaining, the more furious she became.

After more than twenty minutes of discussing this with AJ, Joslyn decided to change the subject and talk about something that could possibly get everyone together and maybe allow them to get to know her, a family dinner. Joslyn knew that AJ would be home in a few weeks, so they decided to plan this extraordinary dinner so both their families could come together in fellowship. Joslyn was still a bit perturbed about the latest turn of events, but she knew that she had to put forth great efforts to establish a relationship with his family.

Joslyn and AJ finished discussing the preliminary ideas that they had come up with and hung up just as she was walking inside their home. Jayla was on the couch reading her history book, listening to her iPod, watching Sister, Sister and texting when she looked back to tell Joslyn that she had eaten a ham sandwich with oodles and noodles, and there was no need to fix anything for dinner. Joslyn asked how her day was and she mumbled as most teenagers do and continued to multitask with reading, listening, watching and texting. Joslyn was always amazed at how teenagers could do all those things at the same time and could tell what was happening with each of them. Joslyn told Jayla that she loved her and was going to take a hot bubble bath and go straight to bed. Joslyn's day had been a doozy and she knew that she had a long day of past messages to review and respond too as well as several clients to see in the coming days. They said their good nights and off to the whirlpool tub with jets, Joslyn went.

The Client List

The morning sun was shining bright and reflecting through the gold sheer curtains that lined Joslyn's bathroom window. Joslyn never needed an alarm clock to awake her as this would most often do the trick. Joslyn lay there for about ten minutes trying to gather her thoughts before rolling out of bed. Joslyn knew that she had to get her messages caught up prior to her clients arriving after lunch; but she was hesitant about doing it. She was hesitant because the last message that she took was that of Abigail's and that encounter was more than she had anticipated. However, Joslyn realizes that she must clear her mailbox because her phone has been ringing non-stop.

Joslyn entered her office and Margaret was busy at work answering the phone, putting people on hold and answering again. Joslyn was amazed at how the influx of calls had been continuous since she counseled Elaine and Dexter. Elaine had informed Joslyn that she would spread the news of her business in hopes of getting her friends and their friends help as well as to help Joslyn's practice flourish. Joslyn thanked Elaine for her support but had no idea to what capacity she was speaking of. Most African American's that Joslyn knew had a stigma about Psychologist and would never think of seeing anyone for help with their issues. However, in their hour of distress, Joslyn has noticed that many were now seeking help because they didn't know what else to do.

Joslyn sat at her desk and dialed her pass code to check her messages. She heard a young lady stating that she wanted to come in for a consultation. The young lady went on about how she doesn't know what else to do with her life. She says, "I've done everything that I was told to do to make him see me for who I am, but he just doesn't get it. She then said, "Oh and by the way my name is Darcie Green and I need to see you as soon as possible because my friend Elaine said that you could help me through my madness. I don't have a number were you can call me back, but you can email me at DarcieG@orangemail.com. I am calling from my home girl's phone right now and don't want to give that number to you. So please email me as soon as possible because I need to know what it is, I'm doing wrong ok. Once again, my email address is DarcieG@orangemail.com. I hope to hear from you soon." Joslyn was puzzled that someone would call and ask for an appointment and not have a contact number to receive a return phone call. Joslyn sat scratching her head for a moment trying to decide if she should email her right away or wait to contact this potential client later. After a few moments, she decided to open her g-mail account and send DarcieG@orangemail.com a message. Joslyn typed:

> *Hi Darcie,*
>
> *This is Joslyn Richardson. I received your message requesting a consultation as soon as possible. There is not a charge for the initial visit because I like to speak with my potential clients first to see if this is the avenue that they are sincere about taking. I will allot a 30 minutes time frame to have a discussion with you about what is happening. If you can, I have an opening this afternoon around 4. I would love to speak with you.*
>
> *Kind Regards,*
>
> *Joslyn Richardson, Ph.D.*

Joslyn sent the email and continued retrieving the messages from her voice mail. Joslyn heard yet another woman named Ramona Perez requesting a meeting with her. Ramona didn't go into any details about what was happening in her life but wanted a meeting as soon as possible. Ramona then paused for a few seconds as if she was unsure of what to say next, and then she continued by leaving her number and a time that was convenient for Joslyn to call back.

Joslyn had taken down this information to have on hand when she returned the call as she always did. Joslyn called Ramona back to schedule her appointment and she answered the phone on the first ring. Joslyn began by introducing herself and then asked Ramona "what can I do to assist you?" Ramona thanked Joslyn for calling back in a timely manner and told her that she would rather discuss her issues in person. Joslyn said, "Okay" and asked if she could also come in later that afternoon for a consultation around 4:30." Ramona was ecstatic that she was able to get an appointment so quickly because most times she would have to wait at least a week to have an appointment of any kind. Ramona agreed and Joslyn told her that she looked forward to their meeting.

Joslyn continued to review the messages left on her voice mail and the ones that Margaret had written down. Most of them regarded confirming appointment, asking for donations or asking her to take part in some charitable event or another, apart from the very last message. The last message that Joslyn heard was from a Xanthia Curtly. Joslyn listened to the message carefully because the young lady sounded as though she was struggling to get her words out as if she was in a great deal of pain. The caller said, "Hi this is Xanthia with an "X" not a "Z" Curtly. I received your name and number from Abigail Weekly, (so that's her last name, Joslyn thought to herself and quickly jotted it down) who is a friend of mine who got your contact information from her friend Elaine. I don't know who Elaine is, but Abigail is cool with her and trusts her advice.

I want to see about coming in for an appointment at your earliest convenience. My number is 555-7575. I will be expecting your call as soon as possible, thanks."

After hanging up, Joslyn decided that she would return her call later that afternoon after she met with Darcie and Ramona. She wrote a note to remind herself to call back while she thought about how many acquaintances Elaine had already told about her establishment. Joslyn knew from her meeting with Abigail and messages from Darcie, Ramona and Xanthia with an "X" that she was going to be booked for the next couple of months. Joslyn would usually start each new client off with a minimum of 2 months with twice a week, 30-minute sessions, or once a week for an hour session. Joslyn was a licensed clinical therapist that could but chose not to prescribe medicine to patients. Joslyn knew that if she went that route and prescribed medicine, that she could double or even triple her earnings. However, she didn't agree with psychologists who gave medicines that only masked the issue/issues that the individual was dealing with, instead of helping sort them out.

Although, there were people that needed to be medicated because of the severity of their issue, Joslyn didn't want to be that type of therapist. Joslyn's approach to therapy was to get the client to see what caused the onset of the problem, the problem itself, what role in the problem was the client responsible and ultimately, a healthy and spiritual resolution for each situation. Although, there were times that some clients refused the spiritual aspect at first stating things like "God would never forgive them" or "Why would God allow this to happen?" Joslyn knew that they felt this way because of their lack of knowledge and understanding of the way that God loves, heals, provides, protects and forgives. However, when they took note that the healing process had begun, they were amazed and grateful that they could see the change all because of God's love and forgiveness.

Joslyn looked at the clock and saw that it was almost lunch time and decided that she would take a nice walk downtown as her office was in the heart of the city. The wind was so cool and crisp; and the chirping of the birds was heavenly as Joslyn walked towards the little park, nick named "Lovers Lane." The park would always have couples eating their lunch, while sitting on blankets, or a young couple would be cuddled up reading to each other. This scene would always remind Joslyn of the love she has with AJ. Each time Joslyn would walk near this park, she would get lost in the moment and lose track of what time it was. She was standing near the railing of the park when her phone rang, and she noticed that it was Margaret calling her from the office. Margaret simply wanted to remind Joslyn that her clients were expected to start arriving in 20 minutes and that she needed to prepare for them as well as review what was discussed at their last session. A good psychologist should always review the conversation from the last meeting prior to continuing with the meeting at hand. Therefore, Joslyn knew that she needed to get back so she could review for the next three clients and then wait to see if Darcie Green would show up at four.

The Mysterious One

It was approaching four o'clock faster on this Tuesday for some reason. Joslyn had finished with her regular clients and patiently awaited Darcie Green's arrival. Joslyn was curious about this potential client because she really didn't want to say much on the phone, and she had to respond to her via email. Joslyn's preference was to speak to clients over the phone most often because she could hear their state of mind in the tonality of their voice. However, she wasn't afforded that opportunity; Therefore, she had to wait to meet Darcie in person.

Margaret came to the door and let Joslyn know that her four o'clock appointment had arrived. Joslyn instructed Margaret to show her in as she walked around from behind her desk. Joslyn always greeted her clients as they were walking through the door with a proper handshake and a smile. She wanted each person that she encountered not to feel intimidated by her, and to feel at ease speaking with her. She would always have the scent of Hawaiian Aroma Therapy candles burning in surrounding places in her office as well as the soothing sound of oceanic waves whistling and whirling from her cd player positioned at the top of her bookcase. This always seemed to calm the spirit of the individual when they came into her office. So, she decided to make it something that she did continuously.

After greeting Darcie, (who was about 5 feet 5 inches tall, with black spiraled locks, a medium frame, manicured, acrylic pink and white nails, mesmerizing hazel eyes and very well dressed) Joslyn showed her to her seat.

She appeared to be dressed for business wearing a linen green pants suit, with a cream shell, along with taupe Nine West sling back pumps, and carrying an authentic Louis Vuitton handbag. Joslyn could always observe what each client looks like and was wearing in those few minutes during the greeting stage. Joslyn returned to her seat and as usual got the preliminaries out of the way by asking her about insurance and paying.

After that was discussed, Joslyn says to Darcie as she does to every potential client, "So what brings you in to see me?" Darcie began by saying, "I have tried everything from talking to friends, family, strangers, and actually seeking out a palm reader for my situation, but nothing has helped my issue. I have a lack of confidence in who I really am and as a result I never reveal to anyone, anything that is true about me. I lead a mysterious life with any man that I met. Except for my family and close friends, no one knows me for me. They know about all the fictitious things that

I've told them. I am a terrible, lying person who lives above her means to impress the masses. I con older wealthy men out of what I can get from them to support my lifestyle and then I disappear. I make all these promises to them saying that I will do this or that, but it's all a lie. They wine and dine me and support my lifestyle. They believe that I am a marketing director for a large firm that I never disclose its name to them. They see the way I dress, my physique and how eloquent I speak, and they believe what I tell them. So, it is easy for me to go from state to state and city to city and put on this façade because of the way I present it to them. I am not sleeping with them; however, there have been times where they had given so much that they refused to give any more if I didn't do something with them. I would then have to make the choice to do what they asked or move on to the next destination. I am tired of this life, but I really don't know how to stop being this person. I just want to be real with Darcie Green for once.

Could you help me with this?" Joslyn had been taking notes the entire time Darcie was talking and paused before she spoke and said, "Yes" I am willing to help you work through your issue, but"....Darcie looked puzzled because she didn't expect Joslyn to say that, so she said, "But what?" Joslyn spoke in a firm, but comforting tone and said, "But you have to be completely honest with yourself. You can't be afraid to see yourself in this process, and you have to take ownership and responsibility for what is revealed to you during this process, agreed?"

Darcie had a look of fear like that of a child being approached by an unfamiliar dog on her street that was growling ferociously at her. She sat there momentarily and then she agreed. Joslyn told her that she had to decide if she wanted to see her once a week or twice a week either way, she would be seen for an hour total each week for the next eight weeks. Darcie said that she preferred to come once a week beginning the following week if possible. Joslyn buzzed Margaret and asked her to come into her office. Margaret came in and Joslyn instructed her to take all of Darcie's information and make an appointment for an hour session the following week. Joslyn stood and thanked Darcie for coming in and told her that she looked forward to working with her. Margaret and Darcie started to walk out when Margaret turned around and told Joslyn that her 4:30 appointment was waiting in the lobby. Joslyn instructed Margaret to give her about five minutes to finish writing her notes and she could show the other client in.

Working toward Perfection

Margaret buzzed Joslyn to be sure that she was

ready to see her final client of the day. Joslyn told Margaret

to show her in. As Joslyn was walking from behind her

desk to greet the potential client, in walks Margaret with

whom she introduced as Ramona Perez. Ramona was a

Hispanic woman with all the enhanced features of an

African American woman. She was about 5 feet 9 inches

tall with long platinum blonde hair, lips that resembled

Angelina Jolie but bigger, extremely long eyelash

extensions and nails, breast implants that were too big for

her petite body frame, an unusually atrocious looking

buttock that clearly allowed you to know that it wasn't

natural, and was dressed in a black lined Marc Jacobs skirt suit that gripped her body and stopped mid-thigh. Joslyn greeted her and asked her to have a seat. Margaret gave Joslyn this look of amazement as she turns to close the door.

Joslyn was a bit thrown by the appearance of Ramona because her dress attire gave the appearance of a professional woman, but her everything else stated "Stripper." Joslyn returned to her seat and again as usual she got the preliminaries out of the way by asking her about insurance and paying. After that was discussed, Joslyn says to Ramona, as she has every potential client, "So what brings you in to see me?" Ramona starts by saying, "I would have never considered seeing a counselor before now because I am a person who never wants to take advice from anyone. I've always said this because, how can someone tell me about me when I am the one living in that space and I'm the one in that situation? However, now, I feel so lost." Joslyn was impressed with the tonality of her voice and the sincerity that exuded from her demeanor. Ramona went on to say, "I feel lost because I am constantly doing things to my body to make those things that I feel that are imperfect, perfect and this is the result that you see before you. I was with my boyfriend Ricardo for seven years and we have a beautiful daughter together named Secret. She is the love of my life and I want to be everything to her, but when Ricardo left us for an African American chic named April and married her, I lost it. I began to neglect my daughter, who is now five-year-old, because I am so consumed with competing with African American women through my appearance to prove that I am beautiful too. I am an Airline Flight Attendant for a major airline company and now my job is on the line because of how I look. I constantly get stares and whistles from men of all nationality, but only derogatory comments from women, mostly African American women. According to them, I am only doing this to get their African American men.

My boss told me that I needed to see a counselor for my behavior, or I will lose my job. It is the company's responsibility to try an intervention when one if its employees is suffering from any addiction. Yes, I realize that this has become a form of addiction and I want to do better. But, every time I see Ricardo on Facebook, Twitter, or any social website with April, it sparks me to do something else to my body. Secret is now living with my sister because I am always traveling, and I don't want her seeing me like this. Ricardo constantly talked about my body and how he wished that I had this or that. He said that he loved me for who I was; but he would insist on me getting things done, but I refused because it wasn't natural. About three years ago he decided that I didn't love him enough to do it and then he left me for a black woman that naturally had all the features that he wanted me to get surgery to enhance. I was devastated because I loved him so much and I thought that we would be a happy family. So, when he left and said that he was done with me and Secret, I was furious. I started working a lot more, taking back to back flights to get the money to take care of Secret and to have those enhancements done. I didn't realize how obsessive it had become until recently I looked in the mirror and was horrified at what I had done to myself. I feel lost now because I have no idea where to go from here. I want the old Ramona back that is tucked away inside here somewhere." Ramona was sobbing so badly that Joslyn was at a loss for words.

Although, clients cry in her office all the time, this was more than mere crying. This was a gut-wrenching release of hurt from this woman's soul and Joslyn knew that she had to help her work through this. Joslyn handed her some Kleenex and waited for her to calm down before she spoke. After about 5 minutes of waiting, Joslyn finally said," Ramona, I am glad that you decided to open up and talk about this. I know this must have been hard to do and maybe you wouldn't have ever done it had it not been for the pressure from your job.

Nonetheless, what just happened here was a major start to your healing process and I look forward to helping you work through this situation okay." Ramona was able to speak now and said, "Okay." Joslyn instructed her to stop by Margaret's desk on her way out to set up an appointment for the following week and she could decide how she wanted to do her sessions. Joslyn thanked her again for coming in and assured her that she would be okay by the end of their sessions.

Ramona walked out and Joslyn sat and gathered her thoughts. Joslyn was really moved by this client because she could relate to wanting to be loved by a man and to have the one that you loved not to love you in the same way. Most often, as a result of feeling rejected, the woman will start to do things that are out of character because of hurt, resentment and pure rebelliousness. Joslyn reflected on Tristan and all that she had gone through; the feeling of hurt just fluttered her heart. It wasn't the reminiscing of what she had with Tristan that caused her to feel hurt, it was the fact that she saw all this hurt in this woman because of a man that caused her to undervalue herself in such a way that would ultimately cause her to self-destruct. Joslyn prayed for all the women that she had encountered in the past two days.

She prayed, *"Lord God, your word in Matthew 6:33 says, but seek ye first the kingdom of God and His righteousness and all these things shall be added unto you. Lord, help these women in any area of need right now in the name of Jesus. Minister to their broken spirits and touch them in a way that they know is the touch of your amazing love and forgiveness. Lord, please use me as a vessel to reach these women and caused them to see you in all of it, and that You*

may be glorified, in Jesus' Name I pray, Amen."

Joslyn finished her notes from her session with Ramona and noticed on the corner of her desk that she needed to return the call to Xanthia with an"X" prior to leaving the office for the day. Joslyn picked up the phone and dialed 555-7575, the number that Xanthia had left on her voice mail. Joslyn waited while the phone rang one, two, three times before a young child answered, "Hello". Joslyn said, "Hello" and asked if she could speak to Xanthia." The little child's voice said, in a high pitch shrilling tone "This is Xanthia, who is this?" Joslyn says, "This is Joslyn Richardson and I was returning a call you left the other day regarding a possible appointment to see me." "Yes, I left the message as I was hoping to be able to come in this week." "Do you mind telling me what it is in reference too?" Xanthia says, "Well do I have to talk about it over the phone or can I come in to do it?" "You can tell me a bit now or you can wait and tell me later, it's really up to you." "Well, I would rather come in and speak with you in your office." "That's fine, just give me a moment to look at my calendar okay, hold on." Xanthia holds the phone while Joslyn checks her calendar. Joslyn returns on the line and says, "Is tomorrow at 10 am good for you?" "Yes, and thanks for seeing me on such short notice." Joslyn told her that she was welcome and that she would see her on tomorrow, Wednesday at 10am.

Joslyn penciled Xanthia in her calendar and noticed that she didn't have many clients on Wednesday, which was almost always the case. She never understood why Wednesday's were slower, but after today's events, she welcomed the lighter load.

I AM NECESSARY – SO WORTH IT

Now the Family Business

Joslyn stopped by China Wok near her office on her way home to get dinner for her and Jayla. Jayla had text Joslyn and told her that if she was going to be late coming home, could she stop and pick her up a small shrimp fried rice, a small beef and broccoli and two spring rolls; and to be sure she got extra soy sauce and plum sauce! Jayla would always text and ask could Joslyn do this or that, especially when it pertained to food knowing that by the time she received the message it would be too late to fix dinner and she would ultimately have to pick up her request. Joslyn didn't mind at times because she loved Jayla and wanted her to have something decent to eat. Jayla would take advantage of this situation because whenever AJ was home, they would have cooked meals all the time except on weekends. Therefore, Jayla would milk this situation every time AJ was away on business. Joslyn didn't want anything much, so she ordered her a cup of egg drop soup and would have a few bites of Jayla's shrimp fried rice.

Joslyn arrived home around 6:30 with food in hand. As she entered the foyer of their home, Jayla rushed her like a linebacker from Notre Dame almost knocking the food and briefcase out of her hands. Joslyn says, "And hello to you too Jayla, how was your day?" "Oh, hi mom, my day was pleasant and how was yours?" Jayla says, as she is rambling through the bag making sure that Joslyn got all that she requested. "My day was very busy with clients and new clients." "Mom, "Yes sweetie" Joslyn answers. "Can I ask you a question? "Yes, you can ask me anything you desire. You know my policy is that no question is a dumb question and you can never get an answer to a question that hasn't been asked", states Joslyn. "Well I want to know; how can you stand to hear all of those people's problems when I know at some point you have problems of your own that you have to deal with?" Briefly, Joslyn thought about the issue that she was having right now with AJ's family and how she should deal with it. Then Joslyn says, "Well many times when I hear the issues of a client, I just listen with an open mind. I know that these people have come to me because they are hurting and need someone that they can confide in to listen to them. My job is to help them filter through what they are going through and try to help them get back to a place of normalcy and growth in their lives." Joslyn continues with, "I am not a magician or anything like that, but I am a person that has gone through many things in my life as a result of destructive behavior. Now that I've accepted Jesus as my personal Savior and has allowed him to purge me of all the garbage, He's given me the wisdom and knowledge to help others that are on the same destructive path that I was." Jayla sat eating her rice before she spoke. After gobbling down several bites she says, "Well I think that it would make me crazy to hear people talk about their problems all day, that's depressing!" Joslyn laughs at her daughter and says, "Yes it does depress me sometimes, but not because of their stories, it's because of how much hurt is embedded in each individual that enters my office." "Well, I am thankful to have a mom that cares so much about me, dad and other people", Jayla says in between eating her broccoli and drinking her tea. "Well thank you sweetie" Joslyn says as she is finishing up her meal.

Joslyn and Jayla finished their meal and Jayla said that she was going upstairs to finish her math homework and Joslyn said that she was going to take a hot shower and wait for AJ to call her for their video chat scheduled at 9:00p.m.

AJ rang Joslyn precisely at 9:00p.m as Joslyn was lying on the bed reading that day's message from "Our Daily Bread". Joslyn would try to read it normally in the mornings, but for some reason this morning she hadn't gotten around to it. Joslyn click accept and AJ was all smiles as usual. AJ was always excited to hear from Joslyn via phone, email or video chat and she knew that by his warm greeting each time she spoke with him. AJ wanted to know how her day went and how was she feeling.

AJ asked how Joslyn was feeling because he knew that the last time that he had spoken to her, she was still so bothered by his sister's drama. AJ loved his family so much, and all he wanted was for them to be happy for him, and for everyone to get along with each other. Joslyn knew that AJ felt this way; therefore, she was so determined to have this gathering to get everyone together for a family fellowship. She was hoping to assure them that she loved him and wanted nothing but the best for him and his relationship with them.

Joslyn says, "Honey I am okay; and my day was a bit busy as I've had several new clients come in today. But other than that, I've had a very interesting day. I also want to tell you how much my practice is growing since one of my clients have been doing 'word of mouth commercials for me." They both laughed and AJ says, "Wow that's great babe, you must have been a life saver for that person because they are out doing commercials for your practice, while chuckling." Joslyn laughs as well and says, "Well she was happy with my service; but I believe that the experience she had with God through Prophetess Gaines is what actually changed her life. However, she still insists on promoting my business and I believe "word of mouth advertising" is the best advertising, so I am grateful for it." AJ agrees and says, "Well be sure that you don't get so bogged down with clients that you lose sight of family because that is first and foremost the most important business off all." Joslyn assures AJ that she knows that family comes first and that she will not bring clients issues home.

Both AJ and Joslyn's jobs require them to deal with the issues of other people. Although AJ wasn't a counselor, he was one of the senior engineers at his company and would have to deal with people and issues all the time. They both promised while they were dating to never bring issues of clients and/or work home and they have kept that promise still to this day. After getting that out of the way, AJ wanted to know if Joslyn had done any more planning to get the families together. Joslyn told AJ that she had spoken with her family and they were all excited about the event and wanted to know when and where. Joslyn told AJ that she was waiting to give her family the exact time and date once he confirmed his flight home and spoke with his family regarding the fellowship. Joslyn says, "AJ have you called anybody in your family to tell them that you were planning this?" Joslyn knew by his silence and the look on his face that AJ hadn't done that yet. "Honey, I want to wait until I get home to tell them of our plans." "AJ why are you asking me about the plans if you don't know they are going to agree because you haven't asked anyone?" says Joslyn. "I told mom about it and she agreed, but she is the only one I spoke with". "Well, I will wait until you get home before I start getting all involved in planning and there may or may not be a fellowship okay!" Joslyn says with a snappy tone in her voice. AJ sensed that she was a little ticked because he hadn't done his part, but he didn't want to deal with that over the phone with his family especially the female ones. The men were always cool with whatever, if food was involved. However, women were not so easily pleased when it came to things that they didn't totally agree with. AJ knew he had his work cut out for him, so he would get on it as soon as he got home.

Joslyn and AJ discussed a few bills, payments and bank accounts before ending the call with their usual smooches and sweet talk. It didn't matter how much they would disagree or how angry either of them got, they vowed to never end a call or go to bed that way.

I AM NECESSARY – SO WORTH IT

Unpredictable and Unstable

Joslyn woke up around five in the morning because she wanted to get a two-mile walk in before heading off to work. As she was putting on her new Asics Gel-Cumulus 19 shoes, she thought about the conversation she and AJ had concerning his family and really hoped that they could come to a happy medium. Joslyn's family was always gamed for a family gathering and a meal; and from what AJ told her, his family was too. However, she hadn't been connected to them in that light yet, so that was soon to be determined, she hoped.

Joslyn trotted downstairs, grabbed her iPod off the kitchen counter and proceeded through the garage for her morning walk. The air was quiet and motionless. The breeze was cool with the aroma of coffee coming from one of the neighbor's houses on her street. Joslyn plugged her headphones into her iPod and Mary Mary's song "Walking" was playing. Joslyn would listen to upbeat gospel music as she walked because this would allow her to have a rapid pace that would increase her heart rate. Joslyn walked for nearly thirty minutes when she noticed she had made it back around to the end of her street. Joslyn would always map out a trail with map my walk so she would know exactly how far she wanted to go. Joslyn made it back home covered in sweat. She left her shoes and iPod in the garage and dashed upstairs to shower and get ready for her day. Joslyn's routine was always Shimmy, (use the bathroom) shave and shower, read her copy of Our Daily Bread, meditate and pray on the word received and then get dressed.

Joslyn came downstairs and Jayla was sitting on the couch eating a bowl of cereal. "Good Morning, sweetie" "Good morning, mom". Joslyn asked if she was almost ready to go and she stated that she was, and they left for work and school. Joslyn pulled up to the drop off area at Jayla's school, told her that she loved her, and to have a nice day while kissing her on the cheek. Jayla says, "You too mom, love you" and walked over to a group of teenagers gathering near the front of the building. Joslyn would watch her for a few moments out of amazement of how grown up she was becoming. Joslyn drove off in route to work with total silence in the car as this was her time with God before entering the office.

When Joslyn arrived, she knew that she didn't have many clients, so she decided to go next door to Mildred's Donut Shop to get a buttered raisin bagel and a small hazelnut coffee mixed half with French vanilla cappuccino. Joslyn sat down and ate her breakfast while watching the patrons come and go. Joslyn enjoyed watching people and would always wonder what was on their minds or what they were going through personally. I guess that was something that most psychologists did to some degree. Joslyn finished her breakfast and returned to her office. It was around nine and she knew that Xanthia would be arriving at ten. Margaret was not scheduled in until nine-thirty because of an appointment that she had to attend too.

Margaret arrived promptly at nine-thirty and reminded Joslyn of her ten o'clock appointment with Xanthia. Joslyn told her thanks and continued looking over some notes that she had written down from one of her manuals concerning behavior disorders. After what seemed like ten minutes, Margaret buzzed and said that her ten o'clock appointment had arrived. Joslyn glanced at her clock and noticed that she had been engrossed in her notes for more than 30 minutes as it was now 10:05 and her client was ready to be seen. Margaret showed Xanthia in and says, "Xanthia Curtly, this is Joslyn Richardson". Joslyn walked from behind her desk and greets Xanthia with a handshake and asked her to have a seat. Xanthia was an African American woman standing about 5 feet 10 inches tall with flawless skin and gorgeous natural hair without the texturizer. She was an average build with blue eyes and pink lips. Xanthia looked as though she was bi-racial, with more Hispanic or Caucasian genetics than African American. Her demeanor was calm and inviting, yet she seemed a little perplexed when looking into her eyes.

Joslyn went through all the preliminaries as she does with all clients to get all of that out the way and then she asked, "So Xanthia, what brings you in to see a therapist?" Xanthia starts by stating that she is a friend of a friend of another friend that she got Joslyn's name and number from. Joslyn was trying to keep up with the friend of a friend thing, but quickly realized that it didn't matter because she knew that the person responsible was Elaine and the rest was history.

Joslyn says, "Okay that's great and I am glad I was able to see you today." Then Xanthia says, "Look I am having problems in my life that I really don't understand. I am this unstable person and I don't understand what caused me to be this way." Joslyn interrupts and says, "what do you mean unstable?" Xanthia says, "Well I seem to go from one extreme to the next, never understanding how I got there. I have mood swings daily and no one wants to interact with me because they say that I am unpredictable and unstable. When I was in middle school, I was diagnosed with an emotional disorder called Emotionally Unstable (Borderline) Personality Disorder. I was bounced around from foster home to foster home, so I never received the proper treatment. Now that I am an adult, I really need help with this illness as I want to lead a normal life." Do you know what this disorder is, and have you had any clients with it?" asked Xanthia as Joslyn pulled a file from a drawer adjacent to her desk. Joslyn says, "Yes, I know what the disorder is, and I have had a client or two with the illness." Joslyn goes on to explain the illness. She says to Xanthia, "Emotionally Unstable (Borderline) Personality Disorder is a condition characterized by impulsive actions, rapidly shifting moods, and chaotic relationships. The individual usually goes from one emotional crisis to another. Often there is dependency, separation anxiety, unstable self-image, chronic feelings of emptiness and threats of self-harm (suicide or self-mutilation). This disorder is only diagnosed when these behaviors become persistent and very disabling/distressing. Did anyone ever explain the disorder to you?" Xanthia says, "No!" "Well, you stated that you wanted help because you want to lead a normal life, what is it about your life that's abnormal?" "Everything that you've described about this disorder, I've experienced at some point or another. I have a promising future in modeling, but I am constantly getting an attitude and blowing up that almost always causes a scene. I can't hold it together long enough to do one photo shoot because the moment the photographer says, "I'm beautiful," I snap. But, when a man that I am involved with who abuses me says that to me, I accept it without any blow up or anything.

 I have met many nice and respectable men, but I run them away because they want to treat me right. I always seem to attach myself to abusers, it's like I feed off the abuse and then I'm satisfied. I guess that's what meant when it says the individual will have an unstable self –image, huh." Joslyn sighs and says, "I have to admit that what you are describing to me is classic for someone with this disorder and in order to get better you have to really put in the work. I have to let you know that although I am able to prescribe medicine for your disorder, I prefer to treat you without it, if you are okay with that." Xanthia says that she is okay with it and agrees to see Joslyn as her therapist. Joslyn buzzed Margaret to finish the paperwork with Xanthia and told her that she looked forward to working with her. Xanthia left and Joslyn was curious about her family and childhood. Most often genetics and what happened in one's childhood is what causes the onset of a personality disorder. Joslyn knew that this would be an interesting case as all the other new clients she had taken on in the past few days.

Joslyn reflected on each of the four women that she had just met and agreed to counsel. Although each of them had an individual problem, they all had two things in common; they didn't like the woman that they were and wanted help to become the woman they desired to be.

I AM NECESSARY – SO WORTH IT

Where to Begin

Joslyn arrived home around 6:30, after stopping at the local Pizza Hut to pick up the pasta dishes that she had ordered for her and Jayla. Jayla was sitting at the table finishing a book that she had checked out from the library, while watching Family Feud, calling out the answers between reading a line or two in the book. Jayla hadn't heard Joslyn come in and was startled when she heard her say, "How do you do that?" Jayla, immediately turned and said, "Mom, why do you always sneak up on me like that?" "Why do you always answer a question with a question? Says Joslyn. Jayla knew that this question for question saga would go on and on if she doesn't just answer her mom and be done with it. She knew that Joslyn was a counselor and that's all she does is ask questions all day. She could not understand for the life of her why a person would pay someone to ask him questions that he could ask and answer himself without paying any money. Oh well, she thought to herself, to each his own. Jayla came back to her present state of mind when she heard Joslyn say, "Well". Jayla said, "Mom... I like having the television, radio, or some type of noise on when I read because it helps me to focus better. When there is total silence, it makes me sleepy or I sometimes start to wonder about different things, and I lose track of what I am supposed to be reading about. I have told you why I do this millions of times mom. Now, why do you sneak up on me so much?" "I wasn't sneaking up on you sweetie. I was watching you as I entered the kitchen, but you didn't hear or see me because you were multitasking as usual", says Joslyn with a smirk on her face. Jayla murmured something with a smirk on her face as well, as she reached for the dishes that Joslyn had picked up from Pizza Hut.

After they sat and ate their dinner, Joslyn decided that she would go upstairs and look over her notes to decide where to begin with counseling her new clients. As she took the stairs to her room, she decided to take a long hot shower, meditate and pray about the four women that she had recently agreed to counsel. Joslyn knew that if she sought God, prayed and meditated on His word, that He would give her clear insight on just how to help these women.

As she stood under the hot, steamy and forceful water pounding down her neck and spine, she couldn't help but remember how frustrated and confused Abigail was about her situation. She didn't even realize how she got to the place of being with her husband's brother. Joslyn knew that this would be a case that was very sensitive because of her feelings, but more so, time sensitive because Abigail was tired of the situation. Joslyn knew that when a woman became tired of a situation, she more than not, would get an "I don't care attitude" and then the chaos and drama would follow. Therefore, Joslyn knew that she had to get Abigail back into her office as soon as possible. She knew that Abigail was a case that she had to really get to the bottom of and fast because her lifestyle had many possible dangers and disasters attached it.

Even though her reflections focused immediately on Abigail, Joslyn didn't take for granted that she had agreed to help three other women, as well as work through her own family situation. Her plate was full now. She already had a demanding schedule, but she knew that these women came to her because they desired change in their lives and wanted someone to steer them into the right direction for that change to take place.

Joslyn emerged from her pensiveness after realizing that the water had turned to drops of cool icicles on her neck and spine. She hurriedly turned the water off and retreated to the warm bathrobe that awaited her near the bathroom door. Just as she was putting on her robe, her husband was calling to check in for the evening. Joslyn picks up on the second ring with a "hey you, how are you?" AJ was always in a joyful mood and responded with "hey you back, I am fine now that I am talking to my beautiful wife, whom I love so much and who loves me back equally as much!" Joslyn was always smitten by AJ's comments as he would always make her feel such love from his words as he did with his actions. She knew that he wanted her to feel his love in every way possible. Joslyn gathers her thoughts and says, "Baby, thanks for always reaffirming your love to me and for me. It is so wonderful to have a husband that gives the 3 P's in a relationship like Steve Harvey says he should". "What is it that Steve Harvey is saying now that has you in this mellow mood", says AJ. "Well, in Steve's book "Think like a man, Act like a Lady", he talks about the three P's. He said a real man will profess his love for her, provide for her and protect her. I just want you to know that you are a real man because you are always professing your love for me and Jayla, providing and protecting us. We are so thankful to God for you". AJ was quiet for a moment and then responded by saying "Honey, it's my job to do all those things. God charged me to be the head of my house and to love my wife and family, provide for and to protect them. I am only doing what God has instructed me to do and I am also doing it because it's who I am in God." "Awe sweetie, you know exactly what to say to make me feel like the queen that I am," says Joslyn.

AJ and Joslyn talked for more than an hour about things to do with housekeeping and then the subject of "Family" arises and becomes the topic of the next hour. Joslyn knew that AJ still hadn't spoken to his family, other than his mother about the fellowship that Joslyn was planning. Joslyn didn't want to get annoyed as she always would when discussing this matter of family. It wasn't so much her family that concerned her, because her family absolutely loved AJ. It's just that everything that Deanna told Joslyn about Larissa, and what she was saying to people about her, kept resonating in her mind repeatedly. Joslyn knew that Deanna was somewhat of a troublemaker too; so, everything that she said may or may not have been true, but one thing Joslyn knew was certain and that is when a person does bring a bone from somewhere there usually is some validity to it.

AJ began by telling Joslyn that he would be home one week before Thanksgiving, which would be two weeks from today's date. Joslyn was so excited because now she could really get to plan the events that would pull both families together. Joslyn then asked the ultimate question regarding AJ's family. "When are you going to contact the rest of your family and tell them of my plans before I spend a lot of unnecessary money?" AJ assures Joslyn that he would contact every one of his family members that he had contact information for and ask them to join us in this fellowship. He went on to assure her that he would have a list of Yay's and Nay's by the end of the week and would forward that on to her.

Joslyn was very pleased with AJ's cooperation with this event. He knew how important it was that he made this happen for her.

AJ and Joslyn talked about a few more things concerning work, bills, said I love you and hung up the phone. After lying back on the bed for a few moments replaying the conversation in her head, Joslyn's mind reflected again on the ladies that she had agreed to help. Joslyn read over a few more notes and decided to call it a night.

She had finally figured out where to begin with Abigail. She knew that there was a deep-rooted seed to every problem and that she had to move beyond the leaves,

branches, bark, trunk, soil, and roots. She had to get down

to heart of the seed that was planted in her to ultimately

cause the behavior. She knows where to begin

now.......The heart of the seed....

I AM NECESSARY – SO WORTH IT

The Heart of the Seed

The weekend had been a very restful time. Jayla spent most of her time in her room listening to music, watching television and catching up on the latest novels that she had checked out from the library. Joslyn did nothing. She didn't want to think about any cases, family or anything. She just wanted her mind to be free of everything for two whole days because she knew that Monday would be the start of new challenges and moments of unexpected truths on her client's behalf. Therefore, she wanted to have a clear mind to process what she knew was in store.

The sound of the birds' chirping outside her window, made Joslyn lie in bed in a fetal position like a baby being sung a lullaby by her mother. The sound was so beautiful and heartwarming. Joslyn was just in awe at how God had created such creatures and how awesome He is in His infinite wisdom. Joslyn continued to lie there waiting for her alarm to chime on in a matter of 30 seconds. She would always awake just before the alarm most mornings because she couldn't stand the sound of that thing going off. AJ, on the other hand, would let it go on and on until Joslyn was frustrated and either nudged him to turn it off or she reached over and turned it off herself. Five, four, three, two, and 6:00, the alarm goes off and Joslyn turns it off immediately. Joslyn sits up on the side of the bed, stretches and proceeds to knock on Jayla's door to make sure she was up and getting prepared for school. Jayla yells from her room, "Yes, mom I am up!" Joslyn knew that Jayla must have heard her door open, because she hadn't even knocked or said anything before Jayla yelled out. Joslyn returned to her room, knelt and prayed and then began preparing herself for her week of opening hearts. Many times, Joslyn felt like a heart surgeon only without the scalpel, blood and guts. Her job does a lot of what a surgeon does when he repairs an artery. A surgeon repairs an artery so that the blood can flow better, and Joslyn helps in repairing the emotional state of a person which is directly connected to their heart in which helps them to function better as well, and as a result causes their heart to feel better. It never ceases to amaze Joslyn how the heart in the surgeon's hands and the heart in a therapist's hands can produce the same results, a healthy heart.

Joslyn dropped Jayla off to school and headed to the office. She arrived around 7:45 to find that Margaret was already in the office with the aroma of a fresh pot of Hazelnut coffee brewing in the lounge, and the soft sounds of Najee playing from Pandora through the intercom system. Joslyn always liked when Margaret arrived before she did, because she would always set the atmosphere in such a way that made you want to escape reality. Margaret was a great secretary and Joslyn never missed an opportunity in letting her know just how much she appreciated her. Joslyn, walked into the lounge where Margaret had her back turned, gazing out the window, humming to the tunes that were playing on Pandora. Joslyn, startled her when she said, "Good morning Margaret, how are you?" Margret jump from being caught by surprise and said, "Good morning Joslyn, I am fine, how are you?" "I am doing great. I love coming to work to an office with such a great secretary; one that thinks it not robbery to go the extra mile to make this place a place of serenity for us and our clients," says Joslyn. "Awe, thanks so much Joslyn, I really appreciate you saying that." "You're welcome" says Joslyn.

Joslyn turned to walk out of the lounge, across the hall into her office when Margaret stops and reminds her that she has a tight schedule today and needed to be sure that no one runs over their time slot as it will cause everyone to have to wait longer for their appointments. Joslyn assured her that she would do her very best to stay on schedule with time. After Joslyn put everything away, she sat and enjoyed her cup of coffee and those few moments of solitude before her first client arrived. Joslyn flipped open her appointment book and noticed that Abigail was her first client at 8:30 for a one-hour long session. Joslyn knew when she saw who her client was and how long the session would be, that she really did need those few moments to gather her thoughts on how she would get Abigail to open about the beginning.

Margaret knocks on the door precisely at 8:30 and tells Joslyn that Abigail, her 8:30 appointment was ready. Joslyn tells Margaret to show her in. Joslyn stood and walked over from behind her desk as she always did to greet her client properly. Joslyn extends her hand and says, "Good morning Abigail, it's great to see you again." Abigail, with a look of distress on her face reaches for Joslyn's hand and says, "Good Morning Mrs. Richardson, it's great to be here again." Joslyn instructed Abigail to have a seat, as she did the same. After sitting down, Joslyn told her that she preferred to be called Joslyn because it feels more personal. Joslyn likes to be called by her first name because she wants the client to feel as though they are speaking to a friend and not a doctor so to speak. Abigail agreed and they began to talk.

Joslyn knew that in order to get to the heart of the seed, she had to start at the beginning. "So Abigail, what was it about Roy that made you jump at the chance to marry him?" Well, can I start at the beginning?" "There is no better place to start, then right there." "Well, first my dad left my mom when I was only five years old. My mom, my sister Trina and I were left all alone. As I said, I was five and my sister Trina was only eight. My dad left because he had grown fond of the woman that ran the club called "Ebony and Ivory" off Highway Five. I never knew what the woman's name was. All I knew is that my mom called her "that thing!" I didn't quite know what "that thing" was at the time, but now I know that it's what some women call the other woman. Anyway, after he was gone for about six months, I guess my mother got into this habit of going out with her friends on Friday and Saturday nights. They would go out drinking and dancing week after week; and week after week, my mother would have a different man, we called "Uncle Somebody", whatever his name was. I didn't know any better, but Trina would always say that mom was being used up by all those men and that they didn't help her with anything. After several years of this behavior, mom finally decided that she was tired and just became a recluse. She just went to work, made sure that we had what we needed and would stay in her room crying most days. I would knock on her door and she would answer only to tell me that she was okay and to go and watch television. I would always obey my mother because I knew what would happen if I didn't."

"Trina was now about 15 years old; I was 12 and my mother was still doing the same things. The only thing that was different was the fact that she finally stopped crying. Trina had started sneaking boys into her room all times of night. I really wanted to tell mother about it, but I didn't want Trina mad at me, so I reluctantly kept my mouth closed. I didn't say anything to mother until I noticed that Trina started to skip school as well, and then I told because school was very important. As it turned out, Trina was now expecting a baby and didn't know who exactly the father was and decided to skip school to try to seek out help from organizations that she had read about. Mother was furious, and as a result she sent Trina off to this school for young pregnant mothers, called GGandG. (God, Girls and Gifts). This organization was a place to encourage the teenager first not to have an abortion and to recognize that a child is a gift.

"Trina was gone for nearly 2 months before mother and I went to visit. Trina was about four months now and was really looking good. Mother had to go in the office and speak with the head counselor and I had a chance to speak with Trina alone. Trina told me that she had become just like mom. She was being with this boy and that boy for whatever reason. She really didn't know why she did what she was doing but did it anyway. She told me not to let a boy take advantage of me and not provide for me. Well, as time went on, I found myself doing exactly what Trina and my mother had done. I was being used up as well. However, one day, I said enough was enough. This is when I stopped dating and became somewhat of a recluse myself;

just as mom had, apart from the crying and staying locked in my room.

What I did instead was made sure that the next man I was involved with was someone that made it totally about me. Roy did exactly that. He made it all about me. He pampered and spoiled me. He made me finally feel like somebody special. He never pressured me for my body, and he did everything for me. He asked me to marry him and I didn't hesitate because I felt that I had finally arrived, and this was a God sent man to me. We were married and life was great until I wanted to do something for myself. You see, I didn't work and Roy didn't want me too. I thought that was a good thing in the beginning until I realized that Roy wanted it that way. He wanted me totally dependent upon him. It gave him some sense of power or something I'm guessing. I quickly became miserable in the marriage because I started to lose sight of who Abigail was. Anyway, after being married to Roy for more than 5 years, he finally decided to go to the family reunion that we had been invited to every year. This is where I met Ron and we hit it off immediately. Ron didn't know me, but after having a conversation with him about my dreams and aspirations, he was very supportive and encouraged me to go for it. Ron really tapped into the emotional part of me and that's why I am in this mess now!" says Abigail. "Wow that was interesting", says Joslyn. "I now have a clear understanding of why you responded to Roy without truly knowing that he had a major deficiency in the area of allowing someone to be an independent person in a relationship." "Abigail, I have an assignment for you to do before our next session. I want you to write down all the emotions that you experienced when your dad left and then I want you to write down all the emotions that you felt when you met Roy and he began to pamper you. I really want you to get in a place of solitude and reflect on both events and tell me honestly what your feelings were. Can you do that for me?"

Abigail agrees to do what Joslyn has asked her too and to have it already for their next session on next Monday. Joslyn told Abigail that their time was up and that she looked forward to seeing her on Monday at 8:30. Joslyn walked Abigail out to the foyer where Margaret and other clients were waiting. She shook her hand and told her that she would see her next week. Joslyn turned and walked back into her office and smiled to herself as she realized that the heart of the seed in Abigail's complicated life was her long-lost father.

Joslyn sat down at her desk and reviewed the other clients that she had scheduled for Monday and realized that she still had to see Darcie at 9:45, Ramona at 11:00 and Xanthia at 1:00. All of Joslyn's new clients were always seen on Monday and again on Friday of the same week if they had 30 minutes sessions simply because she wanted to be sure that they were dedicated to getting the help that they desired. Normally it would be one session a week for an hour or two sessions a week for 30 minutes each session.

Joslyn had about five minutes before Darcie would be

sitting in her chair, so she reviewed what Darcie had told

her during her initial consultation.

I AM NECESSARY – SO WORTH IT

Darcie Green

Margaret knocked as usual and invited Darcie into Joslyn's office. Joslyn greeted Darcie and they both sat in silence for what seemed like an hour because of the suspense in the air. Joslyn began by asking Darcie "How would you describe me?" Darcie replied, "Are you asking me to describe you or who I believe you to be?" "Yes, and yes," said Joslyn. "Well, I think that you are educated, nice, accomplished, and it appears that life has dealt you a pretty good hand!" says Darcie. "What makes you believe that I've had a good hand dealt to me?" says Joslyn. "I don't know. It may be the fact that I see you in this office and it's your own practice. It could also be the fact that you are married and have a well to do husband judging by that 3-karat ring on your finger." Says Darcie.

"Well, I can assure you that God deals us all a perfectly good life, it's what we do that usually changes its shape. Therefore, he did deal me a good life, but somewhere along the way it lost its perfection due to my choices. My life maybe what you see now, but it hasn't always been this way. It really took time and hard work to get to where I am right now." Darcie, I want you to tell me who just doesn't get you and when did you start creating the life that you portray to these strange men? What happened that caused you to escape reality and become a woman that searched out older, seasoned, and wealthy men to keep you, so to speak?" Darcie sat for a moment and began by stating that, "It began when I met my first real boyfriend in high school, only he didn't know it. He was a football player and I was this shy little girl who wore braces and glasses. I was kind and shy, but my family was and is very poor. We didn't have much and no matter how much my mother worked hard for us, we still had very little. Anyway, I was a very honest child and I always expected everyone to be as honest as I was, but he wasn't. He would cheat with other girls, mainly the popular ones and I would see this, but I still wanted him to notice me so badly. One day, I had one of my friends do my hair up, took my glasses off and put on makeup to get him to notice me. He did notice me, only for a split second to tell me that I didn't need to do all that. He said that I was perfect the way I was. I couldn't understand that because he never gave me the time of day. After graduating high school, I had the opportunity to get a makeover by a friend of mine that worked at the mall. Her company needed models for an event, and I wasn't doing anything, so I helped. Well, after the makeover, there was a remarkable transformation that took place. I became someone different instantly. My attitude changed and the way that I carried myself changed. I was always shy, an introvert, but as soon as I walked out on the runway to model, I became someone totally different. After the show, men would come up to me, ask for my number, give me theirs and asked if they could take me to dinner and things like that.

I succumbed into the moment like Miss America sashaying around with her newly fitted crown on her head. I began dating these established men and receiving all sorts of monetary gifts, trips and lavished things that it changed me totally. What really put the icing on the cake is that none of them wanted anything from me at first. They just wanted to have me on their arms. That was fine with me because I had never had so much attention from a man, boy or child before now." "So, basically you feel that being this person that portrays an image of beauty and wealth has been more productive for you instead of the shy introverted girl?" says Joslyn. "Well, Yes! I didn't even get noticed in high school by Mr. Football until I tried to change my appearance and only then did he say not too, and he still didn't approach me after I changed it back. I walked around school my entire high school years just wanting him to say something. Eventually we graduated and went our separate ways and I don't know why I wasn't good enough for him to consider. Now I am this person and I really don't know who I am. I go around from city to city acting like I am wealthy and meet these wealthy men and have them take care of my bills and everything. I don't like being without anything, but I want to be the girl that I knew to be forthright and honest with pure intensions and not this made up life that I have conjured up. I want to be who I was and still feel and be worthy of a man's attention without the entire pretense that I have going on now. How do I do that?" How do I make Darcie Green, Darcie Green again without all the lies and untruths that I've made up?"

"Well, first let me say this to you Darcie. I am a Christian counselor and everything that I do has to line up with what is truth, our truth and God's truth. Before you can truly know who Darcie Green is you must know Darcie Green's truths. When you get to know all of Darcie Green's truth, then you will be able to understand why you are where you are and how you can move forward from that place. So, to begin with, as with all my clients, I am giving you an assignment. I need you to write down all your truths and untruths and bring them back to your next session. Can you do that?" says Joslyn. Darcie, nearly in tears agrees to do her homework and bring it back at the end of the week. Joslyn assures her that looking inside oneself it not always easy, but it is necessary to get us moving from one place to another.

Joslyn shows Darcie out and returns to her desk for another few moments of silence. It was now 10:50 and she would be meeting with Ramona at 11:00 to get to the heart of her seed.

Ramona Perez

It was now 11:00 and Margaret was getting ready to knock on the door when Joslyn opened the door and there stood Ramona with tears already flowing down her cheeks saturating her black Vera Wang Strapless Bustier Dress. Joslyn reached over on her bookshelf and grabbed the Kleenex box and handed it to Ramona. Joslyn didn't have time to really gather her thoughts like she would normally before jumping right in, because Ramona was already in such an emotional state that she needed to know what was happening. Joslyn went over and sat next to Ramona instead of behind her desk and ask, "What is happening right now Ramona?" "Well, I said that I wasn't going to be on those social websites anymore because all they would do is upset me and cause me to harm myself more if I read anything about, or saw any pictures of Ricardo and April. I haven't been on at all since I spoke to you last week until today. Today, I decided that I could handle anything that I read or saw because I felt that I was strong enough to do so until I saw a picture of Ricardo rubbing April's naked pregnant belly on a professional portrait that they had taken together and she posted on his page on Facebook. I can't believe that he left me and Secret and is now starting a family with that woman. How could he do this to us?" Joslyn sat there just listening for a moment and waiting for Ramona to calm down a bit before she interjected in what she was saying. Ramona was really having a hard time dealing with the issue of Ricardo and what he was doing that she couldn't see that his leaving her was a blessing in disguise. Joslyn couldn't wait for the day when Ramona got that revelation in this whole situation.

After more than ten minutes had passed, Joslyn asked Ramona a few questions about herself. Joslyn says, "Does Ricardo being with April upset you because she is African American, or would you be this upset if she was of any ethnicity; and do you believe that Ricardo loves April and didn't love you?" "I am upset because he left me for a woman whom he wanted me to change to become. He wanted me to have more curves like that of a black woman and when I refused to do the surgeries, he left me and his child. I don't know if he loves her or not, but he certainly couldn't have loved me if he left me just like that, now could he?" "Was that a question to me now Ramona? Says Joslyn. "Yes, he couldn't have loved me if he left, right? Says Ramona. "I really can't say why Ricardo or any man does what he does, but I can say that he did leave a remarkable young lady and a beautiful daughter that he had time invested in for a woman that he didn't have that same quality of time invested in because of appearance.

"What I want you to walk away from my office with if not anything else is that, what a person does that he feels is best for his own life, must be okay with the other party or parties involved. I know you are hurting because you think his leaving was about you. Truth is, he left because it was what he wanted to do. He made it about you. He made it appear that way because you didn't want to do what he asked with your body, so he left and went to someone that had what he desired. Well, shortly after he left, you did do what he wanted, and did that make him come back?" Says Joslyn. Ramona sat up straight with a look of disgust on her face and said "No!" "Well, Joslyn says, shouldn't that be a sign to you that you did all of this to yourself because of a man that wanted to go regardless of what you did or didn't do?" Ramona hadn't thought about anything since Ricardo left other than the fact that he left her for an African American woman that he wanted her to resemble. She had spent thousands of dollars trying to compete with a race of women that had no idea that she was competing, and for what? She was competing for a man that was done with a relationship with her and that made her feel that she was less than another type of woman because of her body sculpture and genetic makeup. Ramona began to cry again and this time it was a cry for HELP! Ramona sobbed in Joslyn's office for nearly another ten minutes before she realized that Joslyn had moved back over behind her desk writing something down on paper. After a moment or two of blowing her nose and wiping her eyes, Ramona said, "How can I undo all this, Joslyn?" How can I undo my appearance? How can I undo what I have done to my daughter Secret and most of all, how can I stop loving a man that clearly wasn't the right man in the first place?" "First of all, I have written down a few plastic surgeons here that are very good in the business. You can call them and set up a consultation to see if you can undo some of the work that you've had done.

Secondly, I would like to have some sessions with you and Secret. And finally, I want you to know that getting someone out of your system that you truly loved takes time and work okay." Ramona smiles and stands to leave but stopped to really thank Joslyn for listening. Ramona stated that she hadn't felt that great about her life in a long time and that she owed it all to Joslyn for allowing her to talk and she listened. Joslyn gave Ramona the contact information for the plastic surgeons, shook her hand and told her that she looked forward to meeting little Ms. Secret in their next session.

Ramona walked out and Joslyn rested back in her chair as she starred out the window thinking how women give so much power to the men in their lives. She was engrossed in deep thought when she turned to see Margaret standing at the door asking what she wanted for lunch.

Xanthia Curtly

Lunch was finally over and Joslyn's last client for the day was coming in shortly for her first visit since the initial consultation. Xanthia Curtly was the client that has the personality disorder and really wanted help in dealing with her issues as Joslyn reviewed. Joslyn knew that this case would be one that she had to be sensitive with because it didn't take much to set a person off that had this disorder.

Margaret knocked on the door to advise Joslyn that Xanthia was in the waiting area and was acting a bit peculiar. Joslyn asked Margaret in what way did she feel that she was acting a bit peculiar. Margaret says, "She is sitting there talking to herself and answering her own questions. Not to mention, she has a look of disgust on her face that clearly says that she is upset about something."

"Ok", says Joslyn, send her in.

Xanthia entered Joslyn's office looking simply gorgeous. Her model like frame and fresh silk looking skin made her appear Red Carpet ready. Joslyn greeted her and asked her to have a seat. However, before she could get back around her desk, Xanthia started in on what happened to her over the weekend. Xanthia began ramblings on about her weekend saying, "Joslyn is it okay if I call you Joslyn? Joslyn was not one of those counselors that needed a title in front of her name to feel important or to feel worthy, so calling her by her God given name was no big deal. Joslyn says, " that's fine, you can call me Joslyn if that is more comfortable for you or you can call me Dr. Richardson if that is comfortable for you, it's all about what you feel comfortable doing, there isn't any preference on my behalf". Xanthia says,"Ok" and continued talking about her weekend. She says, "I went to an event to model for an agency last weekend and ran into an old friend of mine that I haven't seen since grade school. Maggie Moore was the girl that would always do her best to make everyone feel that they were less than she was. She was my friend, but I really don't think that she was capable of being a true friend to anyone. She was always sneaking behind my back trying to see someone that she knew I liked or cared about. I remember being at her house and her home phone rang while she was in her bedroom and I was in the kitchen. I happen to answer just as she answered, and it was my boyfriend Sedric. They were talking about me and making plans to see each other behind my back. I never told her that I heard them, and I never let on that I knew that she was seeing him behind my back. However, I did choose to not see him anymore, but I never disclosed why. Later, I was seeing someone else and she did the same thing, only this time, the guy I was dating told me that she came on to him, but he ignored her advances."

"Anyway, I saw her at the event, and she has changed quite a bit in her appearance. She has lost a tremendous amount of weight and has done some cosmetic stuff to her face and her teeth. But, the one thing that I sensed that hasn't changed was her manipulating mannerisms. She walks up to me with her demeaning attitude and asked how I am doing and who am I seeing? What I couldn't understand was, why was who I am seeing important to her after not seeing me in such a long time. I immediately lost it and let her have it. I told her about herself from A to Z and back again. I guess I've had that pinned up inside of me for all these years and I went ballistic. It was so awful that security asked us both to leave the event and I may have lost some potential deals as a result of it. That's not all. When we were escorted out, she began telling me about my disorder and says to me that's why everyone that I have been with has left me because I was crazy. She said that my parents didn't want me because I required too much attention and times when I couldn't have things my way, that I would blow up and cause major problems in their home." I was crying at this point and told her that she was a liar and that she knew nothing about my childhood. But, to my surprise, she says that for years she knew all about my childhood because her mom told her about it. "I never knew any of it because I was so young. I just remember being shipped off from home to home and living with several different families that I would be a part of for a short period and off to another until I became old enough to take care of myself. The fighting went on for nearly an hour outside the premises of the Euro Modeling Agency and then she got into her car and left, as I stood sobbing on the curb near the valet parking booth. I managed to get myself together and retrieved my car and headed home thinking about all that had been said to me about my childhood. I am so upset about what was said to me and the way it was said to me", says Xanthia. Joslyn sat in total aw of what was being said to her. She knew that Xanthia had been diagnosed with this disorder but didn't have any idea the level of issues that came with her disorder. Xanthia hadn't shared any of the details other than that she was placed in foster care and went from foster care to foster care. Joslyn gathered her thoughts quickly and began by saying, "Xanthia, the first thing that we have to do is find out why you were really placed in foster care. I know your friend Maggie gave you a version that you have no knowledge of, but that's the only version that you know. So, what I am proposing is that you go back and begin searching out your ancestry. Right now, you have no idea about who your real relatives are. You only know the foster families that you have encountered. I truly believe that this is where we need to start. What I would like for you to do as a homework assignment before our next session is complete a search on ancestry.com." "Do you know that website", says Joslyn? Xanthia nodded agreeing that she knew what it was. Joslyn continues and says that this website can help you in finding out your birth, any marriage and death records that will let you pinpoint the dates, places and people in your genealogy and give you accurate information concerning your history. I believe that if we start there, we can get some of the basics out of the way and really get to heart of the seed as to what the real issue is. From what I've heard so far, the diagnoses that you have been given may have been given to mask what the real issues were at the time you were experiencing anger and other problems associated with that type of disorder. In my profession, I have come to know that if a person is told long enough that they have a disorder, they tend to act in a manner that supports that diagnoses even if they really don't have it. What I do know is that we will get to the bottom of your potential disorder and give you a sense of who Xanthia Curtly is, okay, says Joslyn". Xanthia says, okay and agrees to do all that Joslyn had instructed and stood to leave and Joslyn walked her out and returned to her office.

After reclining in her chair for more than thirty minutes reflecting on the issues of these women, Joslyn knew that the root of most women's problems revolved around a childhood issue or a man. Either way, she knew that women had to understand that they needed to evaluate what is always happening in their lives . She reflected on how women get so caught up in Life that they forget to Live. They take what is dished out and accept it as so, and never look for ways to better themselves or their situation. She knew that her job was to get women to look inside themselves and truly see themselves. They had to see who they were, who they are, and who they wanted to become. This was a difficult job at times because Joslyn had issues in her own life and that had to be her primary focus, but she had to do all she could to help these people that came to see her. She knew that this was her job, but more importantly it was her purpose in life and she had to fulfill what she was called to do.

What Family Fellowship

Joslyn arrives home after a long day at the office around 6:30 to find that Jayla had prepared a meal for them both. She had called the office earlier and told her mom that she didn't need to pick up anything because she was okay. Joslyn had no idea that she was planning to fix them dinner. She fixed a hamburger casserole that consisted of egg noodles, green peppers, red peppers, onions, cheese, taco seasonings, and other seasonings like that in hamburger helper, her favorite dish. She also prepared a Spinach salad with tomatoes, onions and croutons, along with her famous lemonade that she would make by pouring in a half bag of sugar. Joslyn would always have to dilute it with water, or she would end up a diabetes patient for sure. As Joslyn entered their home, Jayla said, "Hello" and took her briefcase and coat and escorted her to the dining area where she had candles lit in the middle of the table. Joslyn washed up quickly and joined her amazing teenage daughter for a nice meal that she prepared for the two of them.

After praying and giving thanks, Joslyn was so amazed that she had to know what prompted Jayla to be so generous and thoughtful. "Wow, says Joslyn, what made you create such a nice meal and such a warm atmosphere for dinner tonight Jayla?" "Well mom, I've noticed that you've had a lot on your mind lately and that you have been overwhelmed with all the new clients that you have taken on. I wanted to prepare a meal for you, instead of you always waiting on me and preparing meals for me. So, do you like it?" "Yes, sweetie, you've done a great job with the meal. Everything is delicious and the table setting is very nicely done", says Joslyn. As they sat and ate quietly, Joslyn knew that she had to get upstairs and get herself together for evening conversation with AJ.

"Apparently fellowship with the family is never going to happen", Joslyn says as she rolls her eyes, while looking disgusted at the phone while talking to AJ. He really tried to smooth things over with her by telling her that there will be plenty of opportunities to get together as a family and fellowship. Although she was disappointed, she decided that she would let it go and let him handle the family affairs as it related to the blended family getting together. AJ went on to talk about work and things that he wanted to do when he arrived home, but never mentioned why it didn't work out with getting his family onboard with the family fellowship.

After speaking for an hour or so about this and that, Joslyn said her good nights to AJ and hung up the phone. The moment she put her phone on the base and began to prepare to read over some paperwork, her phone buzzed, alerting that she had a text message. It was Margaret with a disturbing message. "I KNOW IT'S AFTER HOURS AND THIS IS NOT OUR POLICY, BUT ABIGAIL WEEKLY CALLED AND LEFT A MESSAGE AT THE OFFICE AND WANTS YOU TO CALL HER ASAP @ 555-5655. SHE STATES IT'S A MATTER OF LIFE AND DEATH" ……Joslyn pondered over the message for a moment trying to decide whether to call or not because after all it was after hours and she didn't like taking her work home with her. However, the words Life and Death really piqued her interest and she settled in her recliner and began to dial the number.

The Unexpected

A s the phone began ringing, Joslyn couldn't help but wonder what was happening now? She had instructed Abigail to do her work by writing down all the things that she felt when her dad left and all the things that she felt when Roy began to pamper her. Joslyn didn't feel that those two things were a hard task, so what on earth could be going on with just writing something down.

Just as Joslyn was playing her previous conversation over in her mind that she had earlier last week with Abigail, she heard voices in the phone. It was a masculine voice that was enraged as well as whimpers in the background that sounded like it could have been a wounded cat or something. Joslyn began to say, "Hello" repeatedly to let the person on the receiving end of the call know that it was connected. Finally, after about ten or more hellos, the masculine voice says, "Is this Joslyn Richardson?" "Yes, and who might this be?" The unknown person began to speak and instructed Joslyn to just listen. "He began by saying, "I know that you are a shrink and that you are helping my wife. She told me that she was going to see a shrink because she has unresolved issues with her dad not being in her life and that it has caused and is causing some of her issues in our marriage." As Joslyn listened, she realized that is was Roy, Abigail's husband on the phone. She just continued to listen because she was trained to allow the person that was enraged get everything that he needed to say out of his system and wait until he is silent, or he asks you a direct question. He continued on stating that "She is walking around here having me feel like I am failing her as a husband because I can't help her with this issue, when it's not her dad at all Doc. The issue is not with her not having her dad in her life, the issue is that she wants my brother in her life." At that moment she hears Abigail's cries in the background saying how sorry she was and that she doesn't know what to do. Roy is shouting many obscene remarks about her being a two-timing whore and that she is nothing and that she will never be nothing. Roy continued in his tirade for nearly five more minutes before he drops the phone and Joslyn hears a door slam. Joslyn began yelling, "Hello" in the phone again to be sure that Abigail was okay because all she could hear was crying through the receiver. Moments later Abigail says, "Hello" and asks if she could meet Joslyn as soon as possible. She really didn't want to go out after nine at night, but this was indeed an emergency and she agreed to meet Abigail at the Applebee's near her office off highway 37.

The restaurant was freezing at that hour and Joslyn was glad that she had decided to put on a sweat suit. Joslyn scanned the restaurant looking for Abigail, and she was sitting in the back wearing all black with a hoodie. She waved to Joslyn and she went over and joined her. As Joslyn was sitting down, Abigail began to apologize for her timing and for all the drama. Joslyn told her that it was okay, and that she needed her to start from the beginning. Abigail stated that it began when she told her to write down things about her dad and her husband Roy. Joslyn says "Okay, but how did all of this come about?" Abigail says, "Well, I was writing as you instructed and trying to sort through everything that I have been feeling for years. I didn't just write about my feelings towards my dad and Roy, but I also wrote about my feelings towards Ron. I know you didn't tell me to do that, but I was so caught up in writing that it just came naturally. Eventually, it became a diary about all my escapades with Ron. I wrote all the details of our late nights together when Roy was working late, or the times that we would sneak around and find secret spots in the place where our families would gather to have quickie's. I even wrote out our escapades by describing each event out in details. I would be writing and get so caught up in my writing that I didn't realize how much I had written or what, for that matter. I wrote how much in love I was with Ron because of how he made me feel inside, and how I was treated like I was a child by Roy. I had written all that stuff in the beginning before it became a shrine of my sexual adventures." "Okay, so how did Roy find out about you and Ron?" "Well, she continued on. I was late for an appointment when I noticed the time and jumped up and rushed out the door. It wasn't until I was 30 minutes away from home that I realized that I didn't put my writing tablet back in my purse. I panicked for a moment but realized the time and knew that I would be back home before Roy was off work. I finished up my appointment and headed straight home to get the tablet to put it away before Roy got home. However, as I turned the corner and pressed the garage opener to drive in the driveway, Roy's truck was backed in the garage. Whenever he backs in, that meant he was home for the evening, which was normally around 7ish, not 5. My heart began to pound loudly, the neighbors could have heard it beating a mile away. I opened the door and walked ever so slowly through the laundry room door, as we often did when we came into the house through the garage. As I entered the kitchen, there sat Roy with my tablet in hand and tears streaming down his face. He was crying so hard and literally began punching the table in rage as I stepped in. I didn't know what to do or say because I was terrified. He began asking me "Why?" "How could I do this to him? What does his brother have that he doesn't? I didn't answer and he yelled "Answer Me!" I told him that it wasn't about him, it was about my dad. He yelled some more and called me a Liar and said that he is paying for me to see a shrink and the only thing that was wrong is that I wanted to sleep with his brother. Then he picks up my phone and makes me call you so I can tell you that there is a real life and death situation and how would you handle it. So, I just left the message and prayed that you would check your machine and call back. I am so thankful that you called because after he said what he said to you, he left in his truck. What do I do now?"

Joslyn sat in total awe that Abigail was asking what she should do now. As she sat there pondering her thoughts, she reflected on the many stories of domestic abuse that she had either heard or read about when something like this happens. She gathered her thoughts and told Abigail to find a relative to stay with for the evening and come to her office at nine the next morning and they would discuss the matter further at that time. Abigail agreed and they both left to retire for the evening.

As Joslyn was driving home, she didn't know what she was going to instruct Abigail to do the next day, but she knew who would instruct her on how to handle it. God! She had to go to God in prayer concerning this situation immediately. She always did, but she knew that she needed Divine intervention with this situation as it could possibly lead to a real life or death situation.

Abigail was terrified when she arrived back home. She had decided not to go to a relative's house because she didn't want them knowing what was happening with her and Roy. Not to mention, the way her family would scold her when they found out that she was not only having an affair with his brother, but she had grown terribly in love with him and didn't know what to do about it.

When she opened the garage to enter their home, Roy's truck was not there, so she felt that she would be okay. Abigail couldn't really sleep because she was so upset that Roy had found out about Ron and what would he do to

Ron. At that moment, she knew that she had to call Ron to explain to him what was happening. As she dialed Ron's number her fingers trembled with anticipation of what could be happening. The phone rang three times and then an unfamiliar voice answers the phone. Abigail knew that it had to be the wrong number because why a lady would be answering Ron's phone, she didn't know. So, she hung up and proceeded to dial his number again, being careful to dial each number precisely. After three rings again, the same lady's voice appeared on the phone. Abigail decided to ask for Ron and then ask who this peculiar lady was answering the phone. "Is Ron there?" "Yes, he is, and may I ask who is calling at this hour!" says the lady. "Excuse me, who are you and why are you clocking his phone like you are his mother, just put him on the phone." "No, you're right. Excuse you! I am not his mother; I am his wife and the mother of his six-month-old twin girls. "What!" Screams Abigail. "Ma'am I don't know who you are and what you want but let me get my husband so he can help you out. Ron gets on the phone not aware of what has happened thus far and says, "Hello, this is Ron, what's going on?" "What do you mean, what is going on? Why didn't you tell me you had a wife and two new babies? Why have you been spending time with me and sleeping with your brother's wife when all along you've got a wife of your own? "Ma'am I think you got me confused with someone else. I think you have the wrong number!" Ron hangs up the phone and now Abigail is at a loss of words, emotions, energy, and most of all hope in any type of real relationship with anyone.

DARCIE'S TRUTHS AND UNTRUTHS

It was late, but Darcie decided to sit and reflect on her life and start the homework that Joslyn had instructed her to do. She has so many truths and untruths that she had to deal with. She first had to deal with all the truths in her life. She came from a poor family. She had felt rejected most of her life by the male counterparts. She desires to have so much than what she has, and she would do anything to have it. She was an extremely convincing liar and she could con well. She uses men, especially older men to get what she wanted out of life. These were all the truths in her life. Now on to the untruths. She was not rich and does not have a successful job at a major company.

When Darcie wrote these things down, she focused on the word rejected and that was the one word that she knew was the root of everything that she had been experiencing in her life. She had never evaluated her life before this assignment from Joslyn. She just continued with life as she knew it and kept that cycle going. Now, it seems that something in her has given her the desire to change. A desire to want more from her; to really find out who she is as a real person and not this made up person. As she continued to ponder over her life, she decided to write what she saw in her life as a truth as well. She wrote, "Darcie, you a nice young lady, a brave lady to ask for help in her time of distress, and a lady that has the potential to be someone special for real!" As she wrote these things, she felt a newness arising in her and she couldn't wait to share these thoughts and feelings with Joslyn on her next visit.

RAMONA PEREZ

Ramona felt good with her decision to go and see a therapist about her issues. Although, the events of today brought her much heart ache seeing Ricardo on social media with April rubbing her belly of their expected child together, Ramona knew that things would get better. The revelations that she experienced in Joslyn's office were mind blowing. Ricardo didn't even want her back after she had decided to do all the cosmetic things to her body. He really did want to leave all along, and he just used the excuse of me not wanting to do what he asked. It was a hard pill to swallow, but she knew that Joslyn was right with everything that she had said regarding that whole situation.

Ramona had called the numbers that Joslyn had given her in hopes of correcting some of the work. She was being very hopeful because she wanted to return to being just plain ole "Mona" as her family would call her. She knew that the buttocks and breast enhancements were going to be the most challenging of all. Everything else was just a little less makeup, shorter weave and nails, and much shorter eyelashes. After the adjustment of all these things the only other adjustment will be her heart. How would she get that fixed? Even in knowing that Ricardo didn't really want her, how can she get him out of her system?

XANTHIA CURTLY

After leaving Joslyn's office Xanthia decided to get started on her homework right away. She stopped by the library to use their computer to go onto the website ancestry.com. As she was walking through the door, she was approached by an older lady that was just coming from the computer room. The lady asked if she was from around the area and Xanthia told her," Yes" and that she was born and raised in the area by foster families. She stated that she didn't know who her real family was and that she was coming to the library to get on ancestry.com to find out. Xanthia didn't know why she shared all that information to a stranger, but she did. The lady decided to tell her that she was there to do the same thing but couldn't figure out how to navigate through the system because she was not very computer savvy and needed help. Xanthia told her that she could come back over and that they could work on it together as they both were there for the same thing.

As they approached the computer area, no one else was in there, so they had the freedom to talk and discuss the reason they were trying to find information on ancestry.com. The lady whose name she still didn't know began to tell her how she had a baby over 20 years ago that had been taken from her. She told her how she was raped by her uncle, her mother's brother and when she became pregnant, her mom sent her to an asylum stating that she was crazy all because she wanted her baby. She went on to say that she never knew what happened to the baby because the family just exiled her, and she never heard from anyone again.

Xanthia really felt sorry for this lady as she was very attractive but seemed a little despondent. The lady continued to explain that she had been locked away hundreds of miles away for over 20 years and they finally realized that nothing was wrong with me and let me leave. I came back to this town because this is where it all started, and I wanted answers. More importantly, I wanted to find my child and prayerfully he or she is still alive and well. "Well do you have any information on your family that you can give me so I can begin the search?" says Xanthia. "Yes, my name is Elizabeth Curtly, and my mother's name was Minnie Curtly. Xanthia froze at the computer for a split second, but she was able to control the outburst that was brewing inside of her. She knew that this had to be a coincidence. How could she be sitting here with a woman with the same last name and she doesn't know her. Xanthia decided not to say anything and just ask for more information. Elizabeth went on to explain everything that happened with the incest and how her mom had her committed. I wanted my baby so badly, but they didn't want that stigma placed on the family, so they sent me away and I don't know what they did with the baby. "Do you know if the baby was a boy or girl?" "Not sure, because they took the baby away as soon as I gave birth in my mother's room and that was it.

They continued to talk about this and that while Xanthia's mind was going a mile a minute. Xanthia was really intrigued with this lady and they had so much in common with their appearance and mannerisms. She knew that there was something with this coincidental meeting. She told her that she had to leave, and could they meet there in a couple of days. She gave Xanthia her number and told her to call her when she wanted to meet. They said their goodbyes and Xanthia couldn't wait to meet with Joslyn to tell her about her adventure.

AJ'S HOME

It was 12:30 in the morning and Joslyn was waiting at the airport to greet AJ as he walked off the plane. She couldn't help but think about all the drama surrounding his sister Larissa and all that she was trying to do. Joslyn knew that she was going to get the family together even if it meant that she had to do it without the help of AJ.

AJ and Joslyn picked up his luggage from baggage claim and headed home. They would always make their pit stop at IHOP to have breakfast and catch up on what was going on since their last conversation. Joslyn and AJ never really discussed work issues because it was a rule that they had set early on in their relationship; however, she had to tell him a little about her new clients without going into full details about anyone on a personal level. They talked about this and that over their meal and retreated home for their usual welcome home escapade.

Joslyn knew that she had to be in the office by nine because she was expecting Abigail to show up, after she hastily told her too last night after the issue with Roy. She told AJ that she had to go in for that appointment and that she would be back home to continue where they left off.

Joslyn arrived at the office around 8:30. There wasn't a single car in the parking lot, not even Margaret's. Joslyn proceeded inside, got a cup of coffee, and sat waiting for Margaret and Abigail to show up. As Joslyn sat looking out the window at her garden, she suddenly heard a voice yelling, "Hello" from in the foyer. At the same time, she hears Margaret walking in and greeting the male that had just entered the office. She told him who she was and asked if she could be of some service to him. The gentleman stated that he needed to talk to a shrink and that his name was Ron Weekly. Joslyn listened with her mouth wide open in disbelief wondering what would bring Ron to her office; not to mention that Abigail would be arriving in a matter of minutes.

Margaret took Ron's information and asked if he could make an appointment for later in the week as the office doesn't do walk in visits. Ron insisted that he couldn't wait and wanted to know if he could see Joslyn some time during that day. Margaret told him to have a seat and she would check to see if Joslyn would make an exception for his sense of emergency.

Joslyn had counseled several male clients, but most of their issues had to do with them going through some sort of mid-life crisis or something. Joslyn knew that if she counseled both Ron and Abigail, it could possibly mean trouble, because they may run into each other. However,

Joslyn was a professional and would never turn a potential male client away, especially this one. Joslyn told Margaret to schedule him for noon and that she would see him for approximately 30 minutes because that's all the time she would allow for a consultation.

Ron agreed to the appointment and left about five till nine. Joslyn was praying that he and Abigail didn't run into each other in the parking lot.

It is now nine and Abigail hasn't shown up. Joslyn began to get a little fearful because of all the things that had gone on the night before. Joslyn instructed Margaret to check the messages and emails to see if Abigail had called or emailed her cancelling the appointment. Margaret check the email and nothing. Then, she dialed the voicemail and hears Abigail weeping and cancelling the session she had at nine. Abigail didn't go into any details, she stated that she was tired and needed to think some things through. Joslyn was okay with that and decided that she would have

Margaret call Ron back to see if he could come on in, so she could see him earlier. Joslyn wanted to get home to AJ as soon as she possibly could.

Ron was back in the office within minutes, looking jolted. Joslyn had a little bit of information about Ron because Abigail was in love with him, and his twin brother had just found out about them the night before. Joslyn would never let Ron know that she had some idea of why he would be at her office.

Margaret showed Ron in. Joslyn went through the preliminaries and asked Ron what brings him in. Ron began by telling her that he had started a relationship with his twin brother's wife more than four years ago, and that he loved her. He also told her that he was in love with his wife of ten years as well. Joslyn was shocked to learn that Ron had a wife. How could he be having this affair with his brother's wife and he is married as well. Joslyn gathered her thoughts and continued listening to what Ron had to say. He told how Abigail had called him last night and his wife answered. She found out that he was married and was devastated. He also said, that he told his wife that the person who called had the wrong number so she wouldn't find out that he was having an affair; because he didn't want to hurt her, nor have to leave his six months old twin daughters. Joslyn was in total shock now. Not only has this man been cheating with his brother's wife, he's been cheating on his wife of ten years and has two young daughters at home.

Joslyn continued to listen and then asked, "Why did you seek out a shrink as you call it, and what made you come to me?" Ron says, "Your name is all around town that you are the best shrink in this area. That you don't try to medicate your clients and that you have had many successes in your practice. I only wanted to come to the best with my issues, because as you know seeking help from a shrink is the last thing that a black man would ever consider doing. But I know that I must get my life under control, or I will lose my life and I mean literally, if my brother or wife finds this out." Joslyn wanted to tell Ron that it was a little too late for that but chose to keep the situations totally separated.

Joslyn instructed Ron to start from the beginning so she could get a better understanding of what his needs were. Ron began by saying, "My father was an abuser of women. My mother knew that he had different women, but she would put up with his mess because of me and Roy. She was the best mother that any young man growing up could ever want because she did everything with and for us. She especially taught us about God and took us to church always. As we began to get older, the fighting that my dad would start with my mom grew to be more than I could stand to bear. I just loathed him because of how he treated mom. I promised that I would never be like him. I wanted to be a man that loved his family and respected his wife to the upmost. I wanted to be the one male in my family that didn't go down this road of cheating and being disrespectful to his wife and family. All the males in my family are cheaters. Even though they were taught the right way to be, they did what they saw the older males do. Anyways, my wife and I were getting along great, and I hadn't even thought about cheating on her or anything of that nature, until I see my brother's wife Abigail. It was something about her that made me fall for her instantly. We've been seeing each other for four years now and I think I love her. I don't want to hurt my wife, or my brother, but I can't get her out of my mind. Last night she called me, and my wife answered the phone. This is when she found out that I was married. I didn't think telling her was a big deal because she was married and was seeing me. I don't want to lose Abigail, I don't want to lose my wife, and I don't want to lose my brother. So, Doc, what do I do?"

Joslyn was taking notes as she listened to Ron give her the run down about his life. She always took notes because she wanted to be sure that she heard everything clearly. This would also help her to put everything in perspective when giving her client feedback. Joslyn said, "Well first, I don't usually tell my clients what to do. We work through their issues together and usually the client realizes what is best for them. I have a few questions to ask. I heard you say that the moment you saw your brother Roy's wife you fell for her instantly. What would make you fall for your brother's wife, and how do you expect your brother, or wife to never find this out with you loving Abigail too? Most importantly, how do you expect not to lose someone in this situation?" Ron sat with a pensive look on his face because he hadn't thoroughly thought about any of this until Abigail's call the night before. Ron says, "I don't know how I ended up falling for her. I met her for the first time at a family reunion and we just began talking about this and that. I have never been able to talk to someone as I did with her.. She listened attentively. I totally lost sight of her being my brother's wife. I just saw a beautiful woman that I was able to talk to, and whom I was attracted too. My brother, nor my wife have found out yet and we've been seeing each other for four years, so I am good on that end. Joslyn wanted to burst his bubble right then, but she just continued writing her notes and listening. The only person that I think that I would lose in this situation is Abigail, because of the call last night. No one else knows about her, but now she knows about my wife. I just don't know what to do with this situation!" Joslyn was trying to process what to tell him, when Margaret buzzed in her office stating that Abigail had just walked into the office. Joslyn didn't know what to do. She didn't want either to know that she was counseling the other. She instructed Margaret to reschedule Abigail for later in the day, even though she really wanted to get home to AJ. As

Margaret was getting ready to ask Abigail, what was a good time for her to come back that afternoon, Abigail starts to cry and insisted on seeing Joslyn right then. Margaret was able to calm her down. She told Abigail that she has a client and that she would have to come back later. Abigail was able to take the twelve o'clock appointment that Ron initially had. She left in tears, and both Margaret and Joslyn were both relieved. Joslyn says, "Now, where were we? Oh, I must admit that you do have a lot going on. I know that your desire is to keep things the way they were before Abigail called last night; but let me assure you that things as they've been for you and Abigail, Roy, and your wife is about to change. I say that because Abigail called last night to talk to a man that she obviously has feeling for as well, and his wife answered. She is hurt I'm sure, and you don't know what a woman will do when she's been scorned. I can tell you that her finding out that you have a wife that way will make her bitter. So, we are out of time, but I want you to sincerely think about what is happening with all of this. Make an appointment to see me next week and we can continue from there okay," Ron agreed, and Joslyn escorted him out to the foyer.

Joslyn called AJ to tell him that she wouldn't be back until that afternoon because she had some clients that really needed to see her. AJ was okay with that and decided that he would catch up on some sports on ESPN since he rarely sees any when he is away.

Abigail shows up exactly at noon still sobbing. Joslyn immediately called her back to the office and wanted to know what all the tears were about. Abigail told Joslyn all about the phone call when Ron's wife answered the phone. She was devastated to know that he was married. She began saying that he was a cheater, and a no good for nothing man. Joslyn couldn't understand why she would be calling him a cheater when she did the cheating with him on her husband, which happens to be his brother.

Joslyn was really confused about that. Joslyn told Abigail

to calm down so she could have a real conversation with

her. Joslyn wanted her to know first and foremost what her

views were on this situation. Joslyn usually doesn't give

advice on what to do, or give her opinion on anyone's life,

though she may have one, she doesn't give it; however, this

situation called for Joslyn to be forthright and speak to her

from a biblical standpoint. Joslyn says, "Abigail, as you

know that my practice is founded on helping people using

biblical principles and allowing them to see that for

themselves. I never try to force my beliefs on anyone, but I

do encourage them from the Word of God." You

understand that right?" Abigail replies, "Yes" by nodding

her head." Joslyn went on to tell her, "First of all, I believe

that there are a lot of hurt people involved here, and hurt

people, hurt other people. The golden rule is to treat people

like you want to be treated. Your husband was really hurt

last night to learn that you have been being with his

brother. You inadvertently found out later last night that Ron has a wife, and now you are hurt. The bible tells us that we reap what we sow; this means whatever you dish out, it is going to come back to you, good and bad. The bible also tells us that adultery is wrong. What you are doing with Ron is wrong. You told me that you know that, but you love him. I just want you to understand that no matter how much you love Ron, it will never work between you too because of all the deceit. Not to mention, it wasn't ordained by God. Remember, how something begins, is usually how it ends. If Ron could conveniently fall for you, you don't think that he has conveniently fell for someone else during his marriage before you?" Abigail sat with a look of numbness all over her face. She sat there and shrugged her shoulders like that of a two-year-old not wanting to face up to her wrongdoings. Joslyn told her that she wanted her to think about all that she has said, and they would discuss it more during her next session. This wasn't a regular scheduled visit for Abigail. Joslyn was kind enough to fit her in because of her situation. Joslyn told Abigail to try and stay with a friend until things cooled off with Roy. Abigail said, "Okay, I will go over my sister Karen's house for a few days." Joslyn walked her out to where Margaret was sitting.

It was now 12:45 in the afternoon and Joslyn was trying to get home to her husband. Joslyn arrived home shortly after one and she and AJ continued to get reacquainted, after him being gone for so long. They had a romantic picnic on a blanket in their bedroom and ended up napping for a couple of hours.

Jayla got home from school and was very excited to see her dad. She knew that for the next three months that she would be pampered a great deal, because she was his little girl and he made it a point to do so.

They immediately decided that they would go for a walk and catch up on what was happening at school.

While Jayla and AJ were out, Joslyn decided that she would check her messages to see if there were any updates on Abigail because there had been no sign of Roy since all the chaos the night before. Nothing was on the voicemail and Joslyn was happy that she didn't have anything that would interrupt her family afternoon and evening with her family.

Darcie's Revelation

T he evening with Joslyn's family went great and she knew that she would have to be to the office bright and early because Darcie Green would be coming in around nine with her completed homework. Joslyn really wanted to take a few days off as she had initially planned, but her client's schedule was very hectic. Joslyn prepared for bed because she knew that the day was going to be heavy.

The alarm clock was ringing to the sound of Jingle Bells, very loudly through the bedroom suite as Joslyn and AJ slept. AJ just continued to lay there as usual as if he doesn't hear it. Joslyn had to reach over and turn it off as she normally does. Joslyn got up, look at the beautiful sky and sun that was glaring through their bedroom window, and thanked God for a beautiful start to another day. Joslyn sat for a moment in awe of the beautiful sunrise and reflected on all that she has with AJ. She thought about Abigail and her issues. She thought about Xanthia and her issues, and she thought about Ramona and her issues. As she began to get dressed, she thought about Darcie and her pretense of a life. Darcie had to find out who she was and write some things down to bring to her session today. Joslyn was eager to see what Darcie had come up with.

Darcie arrives promptly at nine and waits in the reception area until Joslyn was ready for her. Joslyn motions for Darcie to come in, and they began to unpack what Darcie had come up with regarding who she is. Darcie knows that for things to be better in her life, she would need to stay focused and complete the assignment.

Darcie began by saying how beautiful she is and how brave she was to realize that she needed to seek help in the first place. As I was writing down my truths and untruths, I realized that I had become a liar. My life has been based on nothing but lies, and why I started doing this in the first place was based off lies. Lies that I told myself and those that others told me. "So, what you are saying is that you've come to the realization that the lies you were told and believed caused you to become the woman that you are?", Joslyn stated! Joslyn, what I'm saying is that from the moment I felt the rejection from Mr. Football, and later had the makeover and was noticed by wealthy attractive men, the lies became my reality! They told me that I was beautiful, wealthy, smart, a great businesswoman and worth it; so, it all became my reality. I refused to remember the girl that my family and friends knew. I desired to be someone that everyone adored, loved, and wanted to be around . So, this person that I had become fulfilled those desires, until I became tired of it and needed answers. "So, is this what the homework assignment revealed to you?" Says, Joslyn.

Darcie began by saying, "Yes, the homework revealed a lot to me. The rejection from Mr. Football wasn't my first rejection. The first rejection that I experienced was from my dad. He was always too busy to spend time with me. He was always working, or out spending time with his friends. He was a good liar! My mom and I barely had the necessities in life for the most part, and he would lie about helping with this or that. My mom did the best she could with what she had. I would long for my dad to spend quality time with me jumping rope, pushing me on the swing at the park, or just reading a simple book to me, but he always had something better that he wanted to do, and was basically never there. When I realized that I had this real attraction for Mr. Football, but he always had someone else that was better in his eyes, it reminded me of how I felt when my dad did the same thing.

My dad put everything and everyone else before me and

mom. So, now that I have these wealthy, older men, who

adore me and want to spend time with me, I know it's not

because of the real me. It's because of who they think I am.

I present myself in a way that is of the same caliber as they

are, so they are intrigued with me, and this way I never get

rejected. When they want something from me that I am not

prepared to give, I disappear on them. The reason I do that

is because I know once I say "No" to anything that they are

asking, the rejection will come, and I will have to deal with

that feeling again and I don't want that!"

Wow says Joslyn! Darcie, you never mentioned in

our initial conversation that your dad was in your life, but

not present in your life. What I mean by that is that you

knew who he was and that he provided somewhat, but he

wasn't present in the home. He was never there for the

emotional support and growth of you or your mom. Darcie started to weep as she answered, "Yes!" Darcie was weeping so loudly that she drowned out the soothing sounds coming from Pandora. Joslyn allowed her to get it out. As she handed her Kleenex, she asked Darcie where is father now?" Darcie was able to stop crying long enough to answer, with his new wife and daughter. "So, what happened to your mother?" My mother died of natural causes, so the medical examiner said. I think she died of a broken heart. When, I graduated high school and left home on my escapades, my dad really left home, although he was never there anyway, and divorced mom and pursued a life with his new wife Kim and his young daughter Foster! I was so angry with my dad that I haven't spoken to him in years. I've never even met my sister. However, my cousins see him all the time with Kim and Foster at the museums, parks, and the movies. He never even asks about me. Darcie starts to cry again and this time she starts to hyperventilate. Joslyn calmed her down by telling her to breathe. Joslyn knew that the end of their session was approaching, but she didn't want the session to end this way. She asked Darcie did she want to continue, or if she wanted to wait until their next session to continue? Darcie agreed to end the session and continue the next session. As Darcie left Joslyn's office still slightly sobbing, Joslyn sat back in awe of what was revealed during this session. If only men would realize that daughters needed them as much as, if not more than sons!

Darcie was the first client of the day, and Joslyn knew that today would be filled with lots of new information and insight because she had given each of the ladies a homework assignment and had instructed Ramona to reach out to a plastic surgeon to see if any of the cosmetic surgery could be reverse, and to bring her daughter Secret to the next appointment.

Little Miss Secret

It's 10:00 am and Ramona was scheduled to come in. No one had called to reschedule so she expected that Ramona and her daughter Secret would be walking in with Margaret momentarily. Just as she was thinking about them, Margaret knocked, and in walked this gorgeous little bright hazel eyed girl, with long black curly hair, dimples so deep that you could sit a coin in, glowing caramel skin, and the most perfect white teeth. She had the biggest grin on her face. Joslyn walked from behind her desk to greet her, but Secret did the greeting. She said, "Hi, my name is Secret! I am (pointing at her mom) her daughter. My mom tells me that you are helping her sort out some things and that you wanted to speak with me."

Joslyn shook her hand that was extended and said, "I am Joslyn Richardson, I am a psychologist and yes, I would love for you to talk to me a little bit, if that's okay? "That's fine, says Secret! They all sat down, and Joslyn asked Ramona did she speak with any of the surgeons that she'd suggested and was it okay to talk openly? Ramona assured her that it was okay as Secret was aware of what was happening with her because she shared everything with her. Joslyn was a bit perplexed as to why a mother would share all the struggles of her relationship with her dad with a five-year old. Joslyn knew that she had no control over that, just wondered why women, often these days put children in grown folk's business. This is one of the reasons they acted more grown up than they are, and she could tell that this was the case with little Ms. Secret!

Joslyn moved away from her private thoughts on that and asked Ramona again if she had spoken with a surgeon. Ramona stated that she had spoken to a surgeon and he said that she could reverse the breast implants by either removing them or giving her a smaller size. He also stated that she could get the implants removed from her buttocks as well. Joslyn was unaware that she had butt implants. She thought she had taken fat from another part of her body and had it injected. Ramona seemed very excited about the initial visit to the surgeon and had planned to take some time off in the coming weeks to get started with the reversal transformation.

Secret sat smiling the entire time. Joslyn wanted to see what she knew about the whole situation with Ricardo and Ramona. "So, Ms. Secret, how are you doing?" Says Joslyn. Secret sits up tall in her sit with her little legs crossed and said, "I'm well!" "So, everything is good with school, your friends, your mom and dad? Joslyn says! Secret looked a bit sad when she was asked about her dad. Secret stated that school was always fun, she loved learning, her friends were great, except Timothy who always wanted to hold her hand at recess, and that she loved her mom so much and that she was her best friend. Then, she sat and said nothing more." So, what about your dad?" asked Joslyn. Secret hesitated to answer, and then stated that she couldn't say how he is or what he is doing because she doesn't see him. "He used to spend time with me when we all lived together and then he left us, and I don't see him anymore." "How do you feel about that Secret?" asked Joslyn. Secret began speaking like that of scorned woman repeating what she had heard from an adult. "Well, it's his loss! I am a special little girl, who is smart, pretty, and deserving of a good life, so if he doesn't want to be a part of that, it's his loss. I don't need him anyway! I don't need someone who doesn't value me and the special person that I am." Joslyn was caught a bit off guard by the sassy tone that Secret spoke in regarding her dad. This allowed Joslyn to know that even though Secret said all of this, she really was missing her dad. She was only repeating what she's heard. "So, if your dad wanted to spend time with you, take you to the park, get some ice cream, go skating, or do any fun thing of your choice would you allow him too?' Says Joslyn. Secret's eyes were stretched with excitement and said, "You mean we could do anything that I wanted to do?" "Yes", says Joslyn. "So, he could take me to the American Girl's store like Jessica's dad do with her, and we pick out all the beautiful girly stuff, and he help me dress my doll and then we go and have lunch with my doll?" "Would you like that?" asked Joslyn. Secret said, "Please mama, please can we do it?" The excitement in Secret's voice caused something to happen with Ramona. Ramona began to cry, and Joslyn buzzed for Margaret to come and take Secret to the lounge as she needed to speak with Ramona privately.

After Secret left the office, Joslyn asked Ramona what was happening with the tears. Ramona stated, "I have been so angry with Ricardo and what he did to me that I wouldn't let him see Secret at all. I told Secret all the stuff that she said, and that dad left us. Truth is, he left me. He wants to spend time with Secret, but I refuse for my daughter to be around his other woman. "So, Ramona let me get this straight. All this time that her dad has been missing from her life is because of your anger towards him and resentment towards a woman you know nothing about? Says Joslyn. Ramona was weeping by now and couldn't bring herself to answer the question. Joslyn knew by her reaction that this was the case. Joslyn usually allowed the client to see the error of their behavior before she steps in and confirms it, but this time she had to speak her peace about this. Joslyn says, "Ramona, you do realize that keeping Secret away from her dad is hurting her, despite what you are trying to convince her to believe. She sees her friend's dad being actively engaged in their lives and she wants that. You are teaching her indirectly to dislike men and feel that she has no need for them. This is wrong, says

Joslyn." Ramona was finally able to speak and said, "I know!" I know that I shouldn't be this way, but I am still very angry. "Why are you so angry?" says Joslyn. So, a man feels that you are not what he wants, okay that's his choice. That doesn't define who you are and is not the end of the world. There are plenty of men out there that would love you for you, but you must be open to it! You must let go of all the anger and allow God to open your heart to change. He will do it if you allow him too. Ramona sat in total silence, and for once she heard something that she had never heard before. She heard that God could change her and her situation if she allowed him too. Ramona asked Joslyn how did she go about getting God to do that? Ramona didn't grow up in a house of faith and didn't know of anyone who had a personal relationship with God, so all of this was new to her. Joslyn told Ramona she just needed to ask God to come into her heart and make him her Lord and Savior and ultimately trust his Word, which is the bible for direction. Ramona said, "Joslyn can you help me do that before my session ends because I am really tired of all the anger, resentment, and stress that I am causing myself and my daughter." Joslyn reached for Ramona's hand and asked her to repeat after her:

Lord God, forgive me for everything that I've said, done, or thought that hasn't pleased you! Create in me a clean heart and renew the right spirit within me. Help me to understand who I am and whose I am. Remove from me anything that will cause me to not walk in your will and in your way. I believe that you are the Son of God, who died for my sins, and that you rose from the grave on the third day with all power in your hands. I believe that you are sitting at the right hand of God interceding on my behalf. Although, I don't know all of what your words says, I will start to search it for its truth. I thank you for loving me despite me and my mess! Guide my steps from this day forward as I make you my Lord and Savior, in Jesus'

Name, Amen!

Ramona reached over and embraced Joslyn in a way that allowed Joslyn to know that she'd received what she said. Ramona said that she felt some sense of relief and that she was going to figure out a way to make this right with Ricardo for Secret's sake. Joslyn agreed that would be great and that she would see her next week.

Ramona left the office and Joslyn felt great about what had just happened in her office. This was exactly the type of therapist that she wanted to be. She wanted people to come to terms with what part they were playing or have played in their situation and find a solution. Not to mention, point them in the direction of the Source of all things, God!

Joslyn had two more clients to see and she knew that they were also going to give some new insight. She checked her calendar and saw that Xanthia was scheduled at 11:30 for a 30-minute session and then Ron was coming in around 2:30. Joslyn had about twenty-five minutes before Xanthia arrived, so she picked up the phone and called AJ.

When AJ was home, he normally would work on the "Honey Do" list that Joslyn had prepared for him. The list would be all of things that needed fixing or replacing. This time there wasn't much on it, so AJ had a lot of free time to nap, look at the CNN, the stock reports as well as analyze the weather. The phone rang once and he picked up on the first ring and said, "Hey You!" Hey yourself says Joslyn! AJ started talking about his stocks, the weather, and sports before realizing that Joslyn hadn't said a word. Hello, AJ says in the phone, and Joslyn answers, "Yes". I apologize for rambling on and on, are you alright honey? AJ asked. Joslyn assured him that she was okay, that she was just calling to say hi, and ask him to bring her a salad for lunch. AJ wrote down the specifics for the salad, said I

love you and hung up as it was just about time for Xanthia
to arrive.

Xanthia walks in the office with a peculiar look on
her face. Joslyn asked, "how was everything?" Xanthia
stated that she thinks she's seen her mother for the very
first time in her life. Joslyn looked at Xanthia, and for the
first time since meeting her, she could see hope in her eyes.
Joslyn said, "Go on!"

Xanthia begins by saying, "actually, I really want to
share with you an incident that happened when you told me
to go to the library and search Ancestry.com. I was entering
the library and an older lady was leaving. We chatted at the
door briefly about nothing and for some reason I
immediately told her what I was there to do. Ironically, she
was there to do the same thing, but didn't know how to
operate the computer. I told her that we were both there to
do the same thing so we could do it together. So, we walked
back to the computer area and no one was there but the two

of us. She explained that her name was Elizabeth Curtly and that her mom's name was Minnie Curtly. She said that she was molested by her uncle, her mom's brother and that her mom gave the baby away and put her in an institution one hundred miles away because she wanted her baby, and they deemed her to be crazy. She has been there for over twenty years. They finally realized that nothing was wrong with her and allowed her to leave. She came back to this town because this is where it all happened. She doesn't know if the baby was a boy or girl because her mother took the baby as soon as she gave birth in her bedroom." Joslyn was stunned by what she was hearing from Xanthia. She knew that today would be filled with some new revelations, but nothing like this. "So, did she tell you where she is staying or anything like that", asked Joslyn? Xanthia didn't have any other information other than a phone number, and a promise to meet her later in the week. Joslyn told Xanthia to meet with her, don't reveal your last name to her yet, and help her with her ancestry first, this way you may be helping you as well. Xanthia agreed to do that and would give Joslyn an update the following week.

It was lunch time and AJ had arrived at the office with all the fixing for lunch. Joslyn didn't have her next appointment until 2:30, so that gave them more than an hour and a half to have a nice quiet lunch in her office. They sat and ate their salads and made small talk. Joslyn wanted to know what was happening with the family affair. AJ finally admitted that everyone was gamed, but his sister. She had every excuse in the book for why she couldn't make it. That was confusing to Joslyn because they hadn't even selected a date to have it. Joslyn knew that this was going to be a major uphill battle if she cared. Joslyn told AJ that she was going to plan a family day and who ever attends does and that was that. He agreed and the planning began.

They were finishing up lunch when her phone rang. It was Ron asking if he could come in at 2 instead of 2:30

because he was worried about some turn of events that had taken place. Joslyn asked AJ if they could cut their lunch short and he agreed. She told Ron that she would see him at 2:00. AJ kissed Joslyn and she prepared her office to meet with Ron.

Ron Weekly

Ron entered the office, face sweaty and flushed! He began pacing back and forth stating that this is a really bad situation. Joslyn tried to calm him down, but he was so nervous. Joslyn said, "Ron if you would like my help or support, you must tell me what is going on. I can't help you because you aren't saying anything." Ron sat down finally and said that he just found out from Abigail's sister Karen, that Roy found out and has left the house and no one knows where he is. She also told me that Abigail was sick this morning, so she took a home pregnancy test and she is pregnant. Oh my Gosh, what am I going to do? Ron says as he began pacing the floor again. First, we must sit and discuss this like adults, Joslyn says. So, please have a seat. Ron sat down, rocking back and forth in the chair. Listen Ron, because I am a woman of faith and my practice is based upon biblical principles, I must speak with you in terms of that, if that's okay. Ron agreed that it was okay. I don't normally give suggestions. I allow the client to come to terms with what is needed for them to do. God allows us to make choices. He gives us free will. With that free will, we can do as we please, but we must understand that there are responsibilities and consequences in everything that we do, good and bad! Once we have made our choices based on our freedom to do so, we must also be ready to accept all the responsibilities and consequences that goes along with it! Are you following me, Ron? Ron nods his head to say yes. You knew that you were married, you knew that Abigail was your husband's wife, and you knew the probability of sleeping with her unprotected could cause pregnancy, right?

Ron nodded again and said, but I didn't sleep with her at any time unprotected!

I was sure to never do that because I didn't want to take the chance of anything happening. I was just intrigued with her vulnerability and her body. Ron, on our initial visit, you told me that you loved Abigail. What are you saying now? I'm saying that I love my wife and want to keep my family as it is. Joslyn was more confused now that ever. She had to find out if Ron was a habitual cheater and if his wife was aware of it. It appears he has done this before, and that's why he is so nervous. Joslyn asked if he had ever cheated on his wife before? Ron held his head down in shame before admitting that he has. He told Joslyn that he had done it more than four times in the ten years that he has been married to his wife. Abigail is the longest affair I've had. I believe it's lasted so long because no one would have ever suspected it! Joslyn was a bit confused as to why Abigail didn't know he had a wife of ten years. He told Joslyn that when the family would get together his wife would be going through IVF treatments or she would be sick from the treatments. My brother knows that I am married, but Abigail didn't because my brother and I would never talk about anything like that when we're around each other. I feel like he didn't do it because he knew that I was a cheater, so he never asked how she was or anything.

Ron started to cry. Seeing this grown man cry because he was afraid of losing his wife touched Joslyn. It touched her because he allowed lust to take advantage again, and now he doesn't know what to do. "Ron, would you like me to tell you what I think? I will only tell you if you want to hear it." Ron said, "Please tell me what to do and I promise to do!" Well, I'm not going to tell you what to do, but I will tell you what I think about this whole situation, says Joslyn. I think that you need to search yourself and find out what you really want. I think once you've done that and realize what that is, you need to commit to that wholeheartedly. I think you need to continue counseling to find out why you cheat as you do. I think you need to find your brother and try and reconcile and apologize for your misjudgment. I think you need to come clean with your wife, and I think you need to be honest with Abigail and tell her that you never had any intentions of being any more than what you were to her. After doing that, I think you need to ask God to forgive you and pray for him to change your heart. Ron this is what I think", says Joslyn. Ron sat in silence just staring at the ceiling. After a few moments of silence, he said, "I think that I need to do everything that you said. I'm just so afraid of what my brother and my wife will do. I can't lose my brother; he is my best friend and I can't lose my wife because she is the most amazing woman! She's gone through so much to give me children. The doctors told me that I was the reason why she wasn't getting pregnant because of my low sperm count, so that's why we had to do it through IVF". Wait a minute, Joslyn said, so Abigail's pregnancy has nothing to do with you? Ron, replied "No!" There is no way that she could be pregnant from me. When I heard that she was pregnant and that my brother knew I panicked but didn't realized at the time that she couldn't be pregnant from me. She is pregnant from my brother. Joslyn had a sigh of relief that came all over her. Thank you, Jesus, she said aloud! So, how should I go about this Joslyn, asked Ron! I can't tell you how to do it exactly, but you must pray and ask God to guide you in this situation. Come clean with God and watch him work on your behalf! Ron agreed and left Joslyn's office with so much uncertainty!

The Family Day

It was Saturday morning, the day of the Richardson's Family Fun Day! The sky was clear with no sign of rain in the forecast. Joslyn had planned a day of family, fun, food, and games. Joslyn and her sisters were setting the food up, while AJ and her brother-in-law were setting up the bounce house, water slide, horseshoe, badminton, volleyball net, tug-a-war rope, table games and the Karaoke machine for the festivities. It was nearly 9:00 am and the day was scheduled to start at noon.

The grill was sizzling, baked beans and mac 'n cheese were bubbling in the warmers, the potato salad and drinks were chilling on ice, the popcorn machine, snow cone machine, and cotton candy machine were all set up and ready to go. The fryer for the fish was ready as well with the grease warming on low so it wouldn't burn. Everything was coming together nicely. The gathering was at the park close by the AJ's parents' house which was good because if his mom started to feel bad, she could go right down the street to the house and rest. It was going to be a great day!

At noon, family from Joslyn's and AJ's side of the family started arriving. The kids ran straight for the bounce house and the water slide. The adults sat and talked, laughing about one thing or another, or they played table games. The favorite of the table games was the Spades table. You could hear lots of laughter and trash talking at that table. Everyone had arrived by one and there were more than one hundred people at the park. Joslyn walked around making sure that everyone was okay and was enjoying themselves. AJ's family was very nice and inviting to Joslyn and welcomed her to the family. It was a great day!

Around two o clock everyone started lining up to eat, so Joslyn and her sisters started to fix plates. Joslyn didn't notice that quite a few of AJ's family had gone down to the house to eat instead of eating at the park. Joslyn was confused by what was happening. She asked AJ's mom did she cook anything and why were they going there to eat. She stated that she hadn't cooked, but Larissa did and told the family that they could come and get a plate. Joslyn was furious! Why would she choose to cook and invite them over on the same day as the family day? What is wrong with her, Joslyn thought to herself! Joslyn didn't want to alarm anyone as to what was happening, so she pulled AJ to the side and told him what was going on. AJ said that he knew that she had done that but didn't want to spoil it for the rest of the family by telling Joslyn because he knew she would have canceled the whole thing. Joslyn wanted to know why she did it. AJ said she told the family that they shouldn't be eating from somebody that they didn't know and that she would cook for them. Joslyn was even more upset as that implied that something was wrong with the food! Joslyn kept it together, but she knew as soon as this event was over someone was going to hear a piece of her mind!

The last bag of trash was dumped, and everyone was gone except for Joslyn's sisters, and brother-in-law. AJ had already made his way down to his parent's house to have a conversation with his sister. Joslyn decided to tell her sisters what had happened. They couldn't believe that this evilness had taken place amidst something so positive and good! They told Joslyn to not say anything to her, just let it go. They said if she doesn't want a relationship with you, that is her choice and you move on. Joslyn knew everything they were saying was right, but she wanted to tell her off royally.

Joslyn and AJ drove separate cars to the park because there was so much to bring. Joslyn went home and AJ was still at his parent's house. AJ arrived home nearly two hours later with the look of disappointment and sadness in his eyes.

Joslyn didn't say much to him as he showered and came to bed. Once in bed, AJ apologized for the drama and told Joslyn that he told all the family that was at the house that he has made his choice. His wife comes before any of them. That if they wanted to be a part of his life, they had better respect her. He went on to say that he told them that you don't have to like her for whatever your reason is, but she is my wife and you will respect her. He said that Larissa tried to get loud and crazy, but he put a stop to her mess once and for all.

The other family members at the house apologized because they really didn't know the ill will that Larissa had in doing what she did. AJ said that he accepted their apologies and he came home. Joslyn felt sad that AJ had to go through that on her account and told him that she was sorry. But AJ said he was the one that was sorry. He should have told Joslyn what she was doing in the first place. They talked about the event a bit more before deciding to put it all behind them. Joslyn said that she wasn't going to try to engage with a person that doesn't want that, and AJ was fine with it.

It was Sunday morning. Joslyn could hear Jayla practicing her solo that she had to sing in church. Joslyn and AJ got dressed and they all headed off to Sunday morning service. To Joslyn's surprise the parking lot was filled with an unusual number of cars. They had to park in the parking lot across the street, this never happens. Joslyn thought what in the world is going on! As they approached the foyer of the church, Joslyn could see many of AJ's family sitting in the pews. Joslyn had no idea that they would be attending service, but here they were.

Service was great, Jayla sang her sweet little heart out and the message was good! The message was "Love thy neighbor as thyself!" The message resonated with Joslyn a lot because that's what she'd always tried to do, even on yesterday, she thought to herself.

The sound of laughter brought Joslyn out her deep thought of yesterday's event. She turned around and noticed that many of AJ's family were approaching her to apologize. Joslyn told them that it was okay, and all was forgiven. She knew that she couldn't hold anyone responsible for Larissa's actions, but the spirit that lived in her.

The Richardson's left church, went to have Sunday dinner at Red Lobster, Jayla's favorite and went home to spend the rest of the afternoon relaxing and watching tv. Joslyn knew that she had to meet with clients in the morning, so she made it an early night.

Abigail's Reality

Joslyn's day started as it usually does! She prayed, read, and got dressed for work. AJ was lying in bed watching the news as she kissed him and walked out the door. Jayla was ready for school and waiting downstairs as usual. Joslyn dropped off Jayla and continued to work.

The aroma in the air was a bit different that the hazelnut that Joslyn was used to smelling. It had a scent of Apple Spice or something like that. Margaret met Joslyn in her office with a nice brewed cup of Apple Cider. Her you go madam, says Margaret! I hope you enjoy your cider. I know it's not potent like coffee, but I wanted you to try it.

It is so good, and much healthier than coffee is. Thanks, Margaret! I appreciate it, and I'm sure I will love it! Who is my first client and what time is it! Margaret says, 'Your first client is Abigail Weekly, and she arrives at nine. It's a little after eight now, so I have time to review, reflect, and drink my cider, says Joslyn. Margaret nodded in agreement and closed the door. Joslyn sat thinking about what Ron had said about the pregnancy and everything else. She knew that she had to be straightforward with Abigail because all this mess had to stop. She realized that all this cheating and lying was the culprit for many of her client's issues and they needed to get a grip on it.

It was nine o clock, and Margaret promptly knocked on the door to allow Joslyn to know that Abigail was in the waiting area. Joslyn told Margaret to show her in. Abigail's eyes were red and swollen from crying. She looked bewildered, and a bit ill. Joslyn asked if she was okay, if she needed some water, or something. Abigail said that she needed her life to be in order. Joslyn asked her what she meant by in order? Abigail said that she wanted the pain and anguish to go away. She went on to say that she doesn't want to feel what she is feeling.

Joslyn told Abigail that she was being too vague with what she was saying and that she just needed to blurt it out. Abigail said, "I cheated on my husband with his brother only to find out that his brother is married with newborn twin baby girls. I felt that Ron was a better man than my husband because he understood me. He didn't really understand me, he just wanted to be on top of me. I didn't know how to talk to my husband about how I was feeling, so I go and cheat instead with his brother, who does that? Joslyn just listened as she vented. Abigail was on a role and Joslyn just wanted her to hear what she was saying. How could I have been so stupid. I would hear my husband talk on the phone about his brother and his cheating ways, but I didn't realize that he was talking about Ron and I never asked. My husband is a good, hardworking man, but I found every excuse in the book just so I could justify what I was doing. I knew it was wrong when I did it the first time, but the thrill of sneaking with him gave me a rush that I can't explain. "Do you love him," Joslyn asked? Abigail said that she doesn't know what she feels other than stupid! Now, I'm pregnant and I don't know if it's my husband's or his brother's. Joslyn acted shocked by the news but knew that it was her husband's and not Ron's, Abigail just doesn't know it yet! "So, what do you plan to do Abigail? asked Joslyn. "That's why I'm here, I need you to tell me what to do." Joslyn had to tell Abigail the same thing that she'd told Ron. I can't tell you what to do, but I can tell you what I think, if that's okay with you. Abigail agreed and Joslyn began by saying, "I think you need to locate your husband and tell him that you are sorry and that you are pregnant! What! Abigail said in a loud shrilling tone! Why would I tell him that I am pregnant, and it may not be his? Joslyn said and it just might be his! Abigail sat and pondered that thought. What if it's Roy's baby? We could start fresh and new. Joslyn interrupted her thoughts to continue telling her what she thinks. "Again, I think you need to locate your husband and tell him you are sorry and why you did what you did. Don't leave any stones unturned. If you want things to be different, lies cannot be a part of any of this. I think you should tell him that you just found out that you are pregnant and it's his. I think you need to talk to Ron and ask him to forgive you. Abigail interrupted Joslyn and asked why should she ask Ron to forgive her? "Abigail listen, a man can only cheat if a woman is willing to cheat with him. You gave him that opportunity. You must take ownership of that before you can move forward. Lastly, you must ask God for forgiveness and ask him to help you in this situation." "Listen Joslyn, Abigail said. I grew up in a house where God was not a welcomed participant. I never saw my parents pray or do anything related to God, so I don't know what that looks like, or how to do it for that matter. Joslyn asked her if she really wanted change. Abigail said, "Yes!"

I want a different life and if God is the answer for me to have

that, I am willing to accept that. Joslyn told Abigail about

how Jesus came and died for her sins, all of them! The past,

present, and future ones. She told her that if she wanted a

new life in him, that she had to seek change and be honest

and real about doing it! Abigail asked Joslyn to help her.

Joslyn grabbed her hands and said if you are serious repeat

after me. Joslyn prayed the same prayer as she had prayed

with Ramona.

Lord God, forgive me for everything that I've said,

done, or thought that hasn't pleased you! Create in me a

clean heart and renew the right spirit within me. Help me

to understand who I am and whose I am. Remove from me

anything that will cause me to not walk in your will and in

your way. I believe that you are the Son of God, who died

for my sins, and that you rose on the third day with all

power in your hands. I believe that you are sitting at the right hand of God interceding on my behalf. Although, I don't know all of what your words says, I will start to search it for its truth. I thank you for loving me despite me and my mess! Guide my steps from this day forward as I make you my Lord and Savior, in Jesus' Name, Amen!

Abigail sat wondering what would come next as she was terrified to know how Roy was going to react when she tells him that she is pregnant.

Joslyn gave Abigail a hug and she left with hope in her eyes. Joslyn knew that truth would make you free. The outcome of your situation may not be what you want it to be, but truth would remove grip that sin has on you!

Joslyn was getting more clients daily all with similar issues of lust, greed, infidelity, and personality disorders to name a few. Joslyn knew that most of these people really didn't need to be paying her money to help them with their issues, although her salary was great, they needed to seek God for their lives. It dawned on her that Ramona, Ron, and Abigail needed a Savior. They may feel that their Savior was Joslyn, but their Savior, is the Lord Jesus Christ!

As Joslyn sat and pondered about their need for a Savior, she called Margaret into her office. Margaret came in and asked what's up? Joslyn asked her if she could find out if any revivals or women empowerment conferences would be in town or neighboring towns soon? Margaret left Joslyn's office, returning within minutes to inform her that a women's empowerment conference called "I am Necessary, I am So Worth It" would be hosted on Highway 27 at the Radisson Inn, in about a month. Joslyn thanked her. Joslyn knew that she had one month to set up the mission that she wanted to accomplish!

Ramona is Making Things Right!

Ramona was Joslyn's next client and she'd hope that she was settled in to making things right with Ricardo and Secret. Joslyn was reviewing her notes when the phone rang. Margaret was on the phone saying that Ramona was in the lobby with Secret, a man, and another lady who is pregnant. Joslyn wasn't sure what that was about, but told Margaret to show them in. As they entered, Secret hugged Joslyn and thanked her for helping her mom. Joslyn hugged her back and stood waiting for Ramona to explain. Ramona started by introducing Ricardo and his wife April. Joslyn shook hands with them both and asked them all to have a seat! Joslyn wasn't aware that

Ramona was bringing everyone to the meeting, but she was sure curious about how this all happened!

As soon as Joslyn took her seat behind her desk, Ramona began by thanking her for helping her throughout her ordeal. Joslyn said, "You're welcome and I'm glad that you are coming along quite well. So, I see you brought everyone with you today, says Joslyn!" Ramona said, "Yes, I did because I want everyone to be involved in this process with me, since I involved everyone in it without them even knowing I did. First, I want start by apologizing to you April for saying all the mean things I said about you without even knowing you. I just felt you were responsible in some sick sort of way for the breakdown of Ricardo's and my breakup! I've come to realize that it wasn't you at all and I'm sorry!" April accepted Ramona's apology and stated that she was sorry for getting on the band wagon with Ricardo about the whole situation because none of it had anything to do with her! Joslyn just sat and let the conversation go on because she wanted to see where it would go. Joslyn knew that real healing takes place when people can own their part in situations and then try to make it right moving forward.

Ricardo cleared his throat and said, "May I say something?" Joslyn told him that she would love to hear what he had to say. Ricardo began by telling Ramona that he was sorry that he took her through all the drama! He began to get teary eyed as he continued to speak. He turned towards Ramona, grabbed her hands and said, "It was wrong of me to ask you to do those things. You were fine the way you were, but because of my immaturity and sick desires, I put pressure on you about something that I shouldn't have. You are the mother of my daughter and I should have never done that to you! You gave me the most precious gift that a woman could give a man, and I've mistreated you and Secret! I look at the damaged that I did to you and it saddens me because I know that I am the root

of your issues! I made you feel like you weren't good enough, and less than, when in all actuality I'm the one that wasn't good enough. I didn't deserve you or your love, and because I didn't know how to accept it, I abused it!" Ricardo began to weep! He continued in a trembling tone that caused him to catch his breath between every word. "I left you and I did this! I didn't just leave you; I left my precious Secret! He turned to Secret, picked her up and squeezed her so tight in his arms and said, " Baby girl, I am sorry! I am the first representation of what a man should be to you and I've failed you! I was wrong to leave you and your mommy because of my own selfishness. I am so sorry!" Secret began to cry and told her dad that it was okay and that she understands.

Joslyn was sitting at her desk witnessing real healing and forgiveness! She knew that their session was about to end, but she had to allow this session to play out.

She sent a quick email to let Margaret know that she would be running behind!

As Ricardo and Secret managed to get themselves together, April said to Ramona. "When you called us and asked if we could meet you here, we were a bit worried of how this would go. We've had many conversations about this whole situation many times. I know that you were very angry, and I really thought that it wouldn't go as well as it did! I am glad that you invited us here today."

Joslyn waited to see if anyone else was going to say anything before she said anything. Then, out of the blue Secret said, "Well I'm going to be a big sister and I can't wait!" Everyone started to laugh, and Ricardo said, "Yes you are, and I can't either!" Joslyn finally thanked everyone for coming, but she needed to speak with Ramona alone for a couple of minutes and asked everyone if they didn't mind stepping out! Everyone got up to leave and

Ricardo stated that he would sit with Secret in the waiting area until she was done.

Everyone exited the room except Ramona. Joslyn began to ask her about how her appointment with corrective surgery was coming along and how was she feeling? Ramona had the biggest smile on her face, which caused Joslyn to smile as well. Ramona began by telling Joslyn that she has both surgeries scheduled to happen within the next few weeks. She stated that the breast surgery will happen first, and then she would get the implants removed from her bottom in the following weeks. Joslyn was very pleased to hear that everything was looking up for Ramona. "Ramona, may I ask you something?" Says Joslyn! Ramona said, " You can ask me anything!" "Okay, I just want to know how you got to the place of calling and inviting them to this session?" Ramona paused for a moment and said, "I really felt that something changed on the inside of me the last time I was here. I couldn't get the prayer off my mind, and my heart was just

bubbling with feelings that I couldn't explain! I had

feelings of sadness at times, but an overwhelming feeling

of joy in my heart! I couldn't understand what I was

feeling, so I went to a bible bookstore and purchased a

study bible. I wanted to look for scriptures on Joy! There

was one that came across that explained my feelings to a

tea!" Joslyn was all smiles because she knew that Ramona

was becoming that woman that God has intended for her to

be and this made her happy that she could be a part of that.

Joslyn said, "What scripture is that?" Ramona said,

"Nehemiah 8:10; "The joy of the Lord is my strength!"

This scripture talked about God's people being on the road

to restoration, like me! It just allowed me to know how

much God is forgiving, gracious, patient, and

compassionate towards me! When I got this revelation

about this scripture, I knew that I needed to make things

right with Ricardo and April. So, I called them and asked if they could meet me here, because I felt that it was a safe place! I really didn't expect them to say yes, but when they did, I knew that God was working this all out! I know I have a long way to go in my walk with God, but I am so glad that I took the first step. That's why I am so appreciative of you and your services because you really listen to the heart of people and not try to push addictive drugs on them! "Well, I'm glad that you desire to walk with God. Just take one step at a time and you will be okay! So, since you are scheduling your appointment in a couple of weeks, do you want to wait to after your post-surgery appointment to schedule your next session?" Says Joslyn. Ramona stated that would be great because she had a lot to do to prepare for her surgeries as well as get Secret accustomed to spending time over at Ricardo's and April's because they will be keeping her while she has her procedures."

Joslyn came from behind her desk and embraced Ramona and told her how proud she was of her. Ramona left the office and Joslyn retreated to her desk. She had gone thirty minutes over Ramona's scheduled time, but she didn't mind because of the results that she saw happening right before her eyes and it was beautiful.

Joslyn was sitting at her desk reflecting on the goodness of God and the benefits of trusting him when Margaret cleared her throat at the door. Joslyn looked up and asked how long had she been standing there? Margaret stated that she had knocked on the door several times with no answer and was concerned so she entered. I've been standing here for maybe 3 minutes or so, said Margaret. "Are you okay?" She asked. Joslyn stated that she was okay! Well, Ms. Curtly cancelled her appointment for today and wants to reschedule with you later in the week because she has a meeting about Ancestry.com! She said you would know what that meant.

Joslyn smiled, looked at her calendar and said, "schedule her or Friday at 9 am if she can make it. If that time doesn't work for her, tell her that my afternoon on Friday has availability as well and she can schedule for either one of them." Margaret had taken down the notes on the availability and excused herself from Joslyn's office to call Xanthia back to reschedule.

Joslyn decided to take a twenty-minute power nap before her next client arrived!

Xanthia and Family?

Xanthia searched through her purse to find the paper that had Elizabeth's number on it! She dialed the number waiting anxiously for Elizabeth to answer. The phone rang three times and then Xanthia heard a faint voice on the phone saying "hello!" Xanthia kept saying hello because she could barely hear Elizabeth. Elizabeth said, "Hello Xanthia, I am in the Library and have been every day since we met. I am talking low because it is very busy in here today and I don't want to disturb anyone." Xanthia said, "I understand. I will hang up and be to the library shortly!" Elizabeth said, "I really don't want you to come to the library to meet me, can we do lunch today around 2pm?' Xanthia was all smiles because this way it would be in a more inviting setting, and she could get to know the person that could possibly be her immediate family. Xanthia came back to reality and agreed to meet Elizabeth by 2pm at Red Lobster! Xanthia was so excited to have lunch with Elizabeth! She hadn't had anything positive in her life in a long time and this seem to be the start of something great!

Elizabeth arrived at Red Lobster at 1:30 pm because she wanted to get a table that was away from the hustle and bustle of patrons coming in and out. When Xanthia arrived at 2 O'clock precisely, Elizabeth was at the table waiting. The waitress walked her over. Elizabeth stood and gave Xanthia a hug! Xanthia was a bit thrown by the hug, because she had just met her, and they weren't even friends quite yet! Xanthia dismissed her thoughts and returned the hug.

The waitress came over and took their orders. After placing their orders, Elizabeth said with a smile on her face, "So, Xanthia, why didn't you tell me you were my daughter?" Xanthia, eyes began to fill with tears and couldn't bring herself to speak! Elizabeth sat for a moment watching Xanthia as her eyes filled with tears as well, and then said, "I was so taken by you and our conversation that I had to do a little research. My good friend Pearl lives a few miles away and I called her to ask for her help. I went to her home and we sat and talked for hours. She told me of all the things that were going on while I was away. She knew about my baby and said that she had been keeping track of you since you were a little girl. I was floored when she said what your name was. I knew when we met that we had a connection, and to my amazement a striking resemblance, but I had no idea that this would happen." The entire time that Elizabeth was speaking, Xanthia was weeping! It had gotten so loud, that the manager came over and asked if she was okay. Elizabeth assured the manager that she was okay, that she had received some news that she wasn't expecting, but she is fine. The manager gave them some Kleenex and walked away. As they both sat in silence for a moment trying to gather their thoughts, the waitress brought their food to the table. Neither, Elizabeth nor Xanthia had an appetite to eat. So, they sat for another ten minutes in total silence processing what was happening.

Finally, Xanthia was able to speak. "I felt a connection to you the moment that I encountered you! When you said your name, I was sure that you were my mom, but I didn't want to get my hopes up, so I didn't tell you my last name. I am seeing a therapist and she wanted me to wait to get more information before I revealed my last name because she didn't want me to be disappointed if you weren't my mom. I'm crying because I am happy, but I am extremely nervous as well. I know that they took me from you and did those mean things to you and that saddens me. I just don't know what to say to all of this! I know I am thankful that you are alive and well. I am thankful that we met the way that we did, and I am thankful that I have someone that I can call family and Mom if that's okay?"

Elizabeth started to whimper like the soft echo of a cat trapped! She was so overwhelmed with emotion that they had to get their food boxed to carry out! Upon exiting the restaurant, Elizabeth collapsed in the arms of Xanthia. Xanthia was terrified and screamed for help and someone to call 911! When the paramedics arrived, Elizabeth was appearing to hyperventilate a bit. They gave her oxygen and proceeded to check her vitals to make sure she was okay. By this time, most people in the restaurant had come outside. Some came to try to be of some assistance, but others came for the excitement of it all. The paramedics took Elizabeth to the hospital. Xanthia decided that she would drive behind the ambulance to make sure that she was okay.

Xanthia called Joslyn as she waited for the doctors to come out and tell her what was happening. Joslyn was in a session, but Xanthia stressed to Margaret that it was an emergency and that she needed to speak with her ASAP! Margaret relayed the message to Joslyn while Xanthia was on hold. The voice that came back on the phone was Joslyn. Joslyn said, "Hello Xanthia is everything okay?" Xanthia said, "Elizabeth Curtly is my mom! We met for lunch at Red Lobster and when we got ready to leave, she collapsed in my arms. The paramedics came and now I'm at the hospital waiting to see if she is okay!" Joslyn was shocked to hear all that was happening with Xanthia in such short time. She was happy that she'd found her mother, but also afraid that she could possibly lose her if the situation that she is facing in the hospital was not a good report. Joslyn consoled Xanthia and told her that she would reschedule her afternoon appointments if she needed her to come to hospital to be with her. Xanthia was so thankful that Joslyn could come and be with her!

As they continued to wait for a report from the doctor, Joslyn asked Xanthia had she prayed for Elizabeth. Xanthia looked bewildered! Joslyn then asked if she wanted to pray for her. Xanthia said, "Yes!" Joslyn held Xanthia's hands and said," just repeat what I say!"

Lord God, forgive me for everything that I've said, done, or thought that hasn't pleased you! Create in me a clean heart and renew the right spirit within me. Help me to understand who I am and whose I am. Remove from me anything that will cause me to not walk in your will and in your way. I believe that you are the Son of God, who died for my sins, and that you rose on the third day with all power in your hands. I believe that you are sitting at the right hand of God interceding on my behalf. Although, I don't know all of what your words says, I will start to search it for its truth. I thank you for loving me despite me and my mess! O Holy Spirit please come like a dove shield and protect Elizabeth Curtly. Cover her wounds with your grace feathered wings, shield them from hurt, loneliness, and sorrow, breathe hope and songs of love within her. Tend with your goodness the pain that she bears and heal now her sickness with your loving hands and care. Please carry her high above until she can see Your rainbow of promise, and that real hope lies ahead. I love her so much! So please help me to be all that I need to be to her and all that you Jesus, would give out through me! Guide my steps from this day forward, in Jesus' Name, Amen!

As soon as they finished praying, they noticed the nurse waiting to speak to Xanthia. The nurse assured Xanthia that Elizabeth was okay and that she had an anxiety attack that caused the episode that she experienced. The doctor has given her a sedative and she is resting. We are going to keep her for observation for a few days to be sure that nothing else is happening. You can come back tomorrow to see her as the sedative is going to keep her out for the remainder of the evening. Xanthia thanked the nurse for the update and she and Joslyn left the hospital to go home. Xanthia was excited and afraid because of the unknown with Elizabeth, but she knew that according to what Joslyn said, "Prayer will definitely change things!" So, she knew that she would be trying to pray throughout the night for her mom, Elizabeth!

Joslyn arrived home a little after 7:00 pm because she was at the hospital with her client Xanthia. She didn't even think to call AJ or Jayla and asked if they wanted her to pick up something to eat, nor did she realize that she hadn't eaten since lunch. As she exited her car in the garage, she could smell the aroma of something great being cooked inside. She couldn't distinguish what the smell was, but it was oh so good! When she entered the house through the garage, AJ ushered her to the lounge chair where he took her shoes off and proceeded to show her to a bath with the most exhilarating sent of aromatherapy, jasmine, and mint! The mint was always added a great touch to a bath because it opened the mind and causes such a sense of escape!

After dinner and family discussions about the day's events, Joslyn was too exhausted to stay up and watch television with AJ and Jayla, so she headed off to bead listening to the sounds of rain as she drifted off into a coma like sleep!

The sun was shining the like the north star through the sheer curtains in Joslyn's bedroom. She couldn't understand why because when she went to bed, she closed the blackout curtains to be sure that it wouldn't happen. As Joslyn sat on the side of bed in deep thought, she could hear the laughter and chatter of AJ downstairs. Joslyn got dressed and went downstairs to find the aroma of sizzling bacon, scrambled eggs, waffles, and the French Vanilla coffee brewing. She had a full schedule, so she gave her kisses, and grabbed something quick and dashed out the door.

Darcie and Forgiveness

Upon arriving to work, Darcie was waiting in the parking lot. She knew that Darcie had an appointment later in the afternoon, so what could her being here this early be about, Joslyn thought to herself.

"Good Morning Darcie, Joslyn said. What are you doing here so early?" Darcie was smiling and stated that she couldn't wait for her session to share what had happened since their last visit. Joslyn didn't want to speak in the parking lot, so she instructed Margaret to phone her 9:00 patient and try to reschedule for a later date since it was a new client who only wanted a consultation. Margaret did as she asked, and Joslyn and Darcie entered her office.

Joslyn offered Darcie coffee or tea, but Darcie said that she was too excited to drink or eat anything. "So Darcie, start from the beginning, what is going on?"

Darcie began by saying that she knew that she had to confront her father soon, so when she saw him at the park with Foster, she knew that it was the opportunity to do so.

"Why were you at the park Darcie, says Joslyn?' Darcie stated, "I went to the park to pray and ask God to provide an opportunity to get this matter settled. I was sitting near the playground area and heard a voice call out to Foster who was over playing with other kids near the slide. I looked in the direction of the voice that was calling out and it was my dad. As I looked in his direction, our eyes locked on each other. I was paralyzed for about two minutes and so was he. I thought that he would walk away or act as if I wasn't there, but he came over to me and asked if he could sit down. I was still shocked by the whole thing and said nothing. He sat down and just began talking.

He said, "I know that I am really late on saying I'm sorry, but I know that I have too. I was a coward and less than a man to leave you and your mother. I was wrong for how I treated her and you. I don't even know why I was such as jerk, but I was. I can't blame anyone for my bad choices but me and I know that you have every right to hate me. I 've wanted to reach out to you so many times, but I didn't want you to reject me. I've seen other members of the family, and didn't mention you, out of fear of what they would say to me. I am so sorry Darcie for not being there in your life and if you let me, I would love to start from now". Darcie sat in silence, crying! Finally, I was able to speak and said, "Dad, I am seeing a therapist about my relationship with you and she told me to pray about it. I have been praying about it! I prayed that God forgive you for what you did to us, and that he forgives me for the anger and resentment that I 've had towards you all these

years. I asked him to restore our relationship and let it

happen at an unexpected time in a place of calmness. I am

crying because God did just that. He answered my prayers.

I am no longer mad and angry at you! I just want my dad in

my life, and I in his!"

Then, he grabbed and hugged me and called Foster

over and introduced us. We went to dinner later that

evening with his wife Kim, who is very nice by the way,

and I had a wonderful time. We've decided that the past is

the past and we plan to move on from here! They are

Christians and have bible study in their home weekly on

Monday evenings. That's why I came this morning to let

you know that I am canceling my appointment and will

schedule future appointments if needed."

Joslyn just sat smiling! She thanked God for being a

God of second chances and for answering her prayers for

their relationship. Joslyn told Darcie to not be a stranger

and she wanted to see her at the "I AM Necessary, so Worth It" conference in about a week. Darcie said that she had heard about it and had already purchased tickets for her and Kim. Joslyn hugged her and Darcie left her office.

Margaret entered the office as Darcie was leaving and smiling as well. Joslyn asked why she was all smiles, and she stated as Darcie was on her way out, she said, "I have parents now!" I felt the joy of that statement all through my being. I am so happy for her. Joslyn stated that she was as well. "Okay, Margaret who is on my schedule next?" Well said Margaret, "Mrs. Abigail, Ron Weekly, A guy that looks just like him, and a lady who looks pregnant just showed up! "What?" Said Joslyn. Margaret attempted to say it again and Joslyn stopped her mid statement. "Who had an appointment with me next?" "Ms. Abigail did, and she brought the others with her." Give me a few moments to get my thoughts together and send them in, in a couple of minutes.

I AM NECESSARY – SO WORTH IT

The Devil Never Wins

Margraet knocked and showed Abigail and the other guests in. Joslyn welcomed them and sat down behind her desk. She started by asking Abigail to begin since it was her session. Abigail didn't know where to start, so she started by apologizing to everyone in the room. She told her husband that she was sorry for cheating and that she did so because of her own selfish reasons.

She apologized to Ron's wife for pursuing a relationship with him. She apologized to Ron for getting involved with him and she was married to his brother. Abigail was saying so much that it was barely understood because she was weeping so badly. She turned to her husband Roy and said, " I am especially sorry for putting you and our baby through this!' The stress of this nonsense is causing me to have problems and I have been spotting the last couple of days. Roy, looked bewildered, and yelled "HOLDUP!" "Abigail are you telling me that you are having a baby from me now?' Abigail, turns to Roy, wiping her eyes and says, "Yes!" How do you know that it's my baby since you have been around here sleeping with my brother right under my nose all this time?" Abigail stands and walks over to Roy who is now weeping too! I know it's your baby because I was never with your brother unprotected and besides, he can't have children anyway." Are you really that stupid to make me believe he can't have children and his wife just gave birth to twins almost six months ago, and she is sitting over there looking pregnant again?' At this moment, Ron's wife says, "She is telling the truth. She is not pregnant by my husband." Roy stands to leave and suddenly falls to his knees in front of Abigail. He was crying, while rubbing her stomach and thanking God simultaneously. Joslyn was moved by what was happening in her office. She just knew that this was going to go way left. Roy finally got himself together, stands and apologizes to his wife for not being the understanding and supportive husband that she needed. I also need to apologize for thinking about cheating because you had done it to me. When I left and was gone all those hours, I had gone to my ex Taylor's house to get with her. She had been trying to get back with me for years and I would dismiss her advances. But the other night, I decided to just show up at her place. She was shocked to see me and asked why was I there? I told her that I wanted to be with her and about our whole situation. To my surprise, she had changed. I hadn't spoken with her in a while, so during that time she had changed her life and is now a Christian. She told me how she could no longer do the things that she had and that I needed to forgive you and try to work out my marriage. She talked about how people make decisions based on the emotions that they are feeling, and in those initial 120 seconds of the initial shock of everything could and would change the trajectory of our lives if we don't stop, breathe, and reflect before reacting. She told me about seeking help from Joslyn to talk through my anger and disappointment. It was ironic that you would call and ask to meet you here. Roy and Abigail was still crying when Ron apologized to his brother, Abigail, and his wife for the role he played. Everyone was hugging and apologizing when Joslyn stood to speak.

Joslyn asked if she could speak and everyone nodded. Joslyn began by saying that she was thankful to God to see that they each were apologizing and making amends with each other. "Can I just speak for a minute to each of you?" "You cannot let selfishness, bitterness, and lust cause you not to honor your commitment to your spouse. You all know that my practice is founded on utilizing biblical principles, so I'm going to give it to you from the Bible. The bible tells us, "A man should love his wife as Christ loves the church.". This means that after God, your top priority should be your wife, and wives your husband. You must honor your wives with the upmost respect. Wives, you must do the same. The devil never wins unless you allow him too. If you leave any open area in your lives uncovered or lacking the word of God, the enemy will come in and try to destroy what God has ordained. Don't be fooled by his subtle tactics. He will do whatever he can to break up families especially marriages. Wives, one of you are already a mother, and the other is going to be mother, you must be careful of what you expose your children too. If you all are going to work on your marriages and if the forgiveness was real here today, you must let the past go and move forward from here by putting God first and trusting him with everything! Does everyone understand what I am saying?" Everyone nodded as to say, "Yes!" Abigail asked if she and Roy could continue sessions with her, as did Ron and his wife. Joslyn reminded both women of the upcoming event and told them that she hoped to see them there. They made their appointments and left the office.

Joslyn had several more clients for the day, but she was already exhausted.

It was two in the afternoon, Joslyn had eaten her lunch and only had one more client to see. She hadn't heard from Xanthia since being at the hospital with her, when her newly found mother fell ill. She didn't know if she was going to make her appointment at 2:30 or not. Joslyn had about thirty minutes to look over notes and review some of the information of potential new clients. While sitting at her desk, she saw on her calendar that the upcoming event "I Am Necessary, so Worth it" would be in town that coming Saturday. She was encouraging her clients to attend, but

time had slipped away from her and she didn't realize that
it was only a few days away, Joslyn sat thinking about her
own situation for a moment. Although many of the family
members had apologized about the events of Family Day,
she nor AJ had spoken to Larissa about anything. AJ had
called several times, but she refused to accept his call.
Joslyn would hear him praying about the situation when he
would have his alone time in their prayer room. Joslyn
didn't mention anything about the events of the day
because she had decided that she would pray and allow
God to fix whatever was going on with Larissa.

A strong knock on her office door took Joslyn out
of her pensive state. She told Margaret that she could come
in. Margaret entered and told Joslyn that Xanthia had
cancelled and that she would see her at the event on
Saturday. Margaret stated that she didn't give any details of
why she wanted to cancel. Joslyn thanked Margaret and
prepared her things to go home. As she was gathering her

things, she couldn't help but think about Xanthia and her mother and how things were going. She wanted to call Xanthia to get an update but decided that she would wait and let Xanthia contact her. She gathered her things and headed home.

I Am Necessary, so Worth It

The rest of the week was as any other week. It was full of potential new clients coming in with many of the same issues, or clients that were still trying to work through their issues. Joslyn was happy that it was Saturday and that she could enjoy the conference and fellowship with many of the women that she had counseled and those whom she had encountered in one space or another.

It was 7:30 am, and Joslyn could smell the aroma of bacon sizzling in the kitchen. AJ was preparing breakfast for him and Jayla because she would eat brunch at the conference that was scheduled to start at 10:00 am. She entered the kitchen and they were laughing and talking sports as they usually did when they were together. Joslyn joined in and they laugh and talked for nearly an hour when Joslyn noticed that time and ran upstairs to get dressed.

Joslyn entered the conference space at Radisson Inn on Hwy 27. The room was filled with pink table clothes and chair covers accented with black napkins with pink, black, and purple assorted flowers and accents all around the room. There were more than thirty women already mingling with each other at the back of the room near the coffee bar. Joslyn didn't really recognize many of the women. There were women of all nationalities and ethnicities. She was excited to see women coming together to fellowship. Joslyn walked over to see who the speakers for this event were. She noticed that Evangelist Stacey Jones and Minister Jackie Russell would be speaking to the ladies. Joslyn hadn't heard Stacey speak before, but she had the pleasure of hearing Jackie speak at an event called

"Tea, Time, and Talk" that she hosted several years ago.

That event allowed women to fellowship in a tea party

setting and share whatever they felt the need to talk about.

Joslyn grabbed her a cup of orange juice and found a seat

near the middle of the room. Joslyn never liked sitting in

the back or front. She preferred the middle area of the room

for whatever reason. As Joslyn was taking her seat, she

noticed that there were a vast range of ladies in the room.

There were young ladies as young as 15 years of age and

seasoned women as old as 80 years of age in the building.

The conference had attracted a lot of women.

The preliminaries of eating, drawing raffle tickets,

and pulling names for special gifts was ending and now it

was time for the word. Jackie would be the first speaker.

Jackie was a speaker who spoke from a place of

transparency. She wanted the ladies to know that it doesn't

matter what they were going through that they could

choose to keep pressing on or give up and allow God to use

their gifts through someone else. Jackie just kept it plain and simple without yelling or anything like that. Jackie wanted the women to hear what she had to say with clarity. As Jackie spoke about her childhood, her broken marriage, her plight with infidelity, adultery, church hurt, and rebelliousness, Joslyn scanned the room and saw many of the women weeping and consoling each other. Joslyn new that this would be a great conference for her clients to attend because many of them could relate with what was being revealed through Jackie's transparency and testimony. Jackie spoke for 20 minutes and there was as 15-minute intermission before Evangelist Stacey Jones would speak. During the intermission, the voices of women praying, crying, and consoling each other filled the room with such a sweet aroma of Love.

After the 15 minutes intermission, the MC introduced Evangelist Stacey Jones. Stacey Jones was ready to feed the women of God what God had given her to minister to the women in the building.

Evangelist Stacey Jones began by saying, *'I am Necessary, and I am worth it!'*

Philippians 4:13 says, "I can do all things through him who gives me strength."

As I reflect on, I am Necessary and I know my worth Conference, I came to realize that I was not always at this place. As a child growing up, I lived with my mother. My father was living out of state and we did not have much of a relationship. As I grew older, I became angry and bitter. I was angry and bitter because as I grew older, I wanted my father in my life. Give me some time and let me walk through this with you.

I do not want to put the blame on my father for not being there, however when I was at a young age, I gravitated towards wanting relationships with older men. I must be transparent to let you know I allowed those toxic relationships to become a part of me. With all that I had going on in my life I didn't value myself, I didn't feel like I was Necessary, nor did I know my worth. To be honest I did not care! If I had an older man in my life, I was good. Keep in mind I was going through this in Middle school! How can a young girl find older men attractive!? It was something missing. I found comfort in knowing an older man wanted me. Could it be I was crying out for a father?

By the time I got in High School, I found someone around my age, and I got pregnant with my first child in High School. I went to school with a "Belly" full of baby. I felt as if I was wanted and valued because I was pregnant, Still not knowing my Worth! I end up marring my kid's father in 1997.

Even after marriage, yet and still I did not know my worth. Let me explain why... I was still holding on to my past and was not fully delivered from it! Now I am walking in a marriage not knowing my worth as a wife. During the marriage there was a lot of infidelity, and my self-esteem was already low. I just thought that the way I was feeling was the "norm". Not realizing I didn't love me! So, if you don't love yourself, how can you be Necessary enough to receive love from your Husband?"

I began to realize that I had to fight through many things in my marriage, all because I had lost my identity from within. I fought through being Lonely, I fought through Depression, I fought through Anger, I fought through Betrayal, and I fought through Rejection. I had to fight through many emotional issues of the heart because of not knowing that I was valuable, not knowing my worth! The fight was Necessary, if it was not, I wouldn't be standing here sharing my testimony. Revelation 12:11 SAYS AND THEY OVERCAME BY THE BLOOD OF THE LAMB, AND BY THE WORD OF THEIR TESTIMONY! Let me just share this with you. You will be treated according to how you value yourself. If you do not love yourself, how can you except love from anyone? The woman with the issue of blood, fought 12 years with the issues of bleeding in her body... (She was considered unclean and contaminated) Back in those days, it was against the law to come out contaminated, with her fight in my spiritual imagination this woman could have felt lonely, rejected, bitter, isolated, weak and feeble with no strength at all. I can see this woman going to the Doctors with hopes to only come out depressed, with her head down. I see her in the spirit as being a prisoner in her own home, and always in a bent over posture saying to herself (No one loves me, I don't have any friends, No husband, no money, I'm tired!).

After reading and reviewing her story, I came to realize that we both went through a time where we had to fight through! Amid going through, God was making Women of God that would Worship him like they had never done before!

Women of God! If you're in a situation that you feel that you can't come out, or you may be feeling that you're not worthy to continue this race that God has set before you... Let me just encourage you to Stay in the race, (ECCLESIASTES 9:11) for the race is not given to the swift, but the one that will endure to the end. Go through the process , because it's in that place God is making the Women that HE has called, BEFORE CITIES, BEFORE

NATIONS, BEFORE REGIONS, to share your testimony for his sons and daughters; so that they will be delivered through YOUR "Process"! If God hides you during a season of your Process, please know that it's Okay!!!! God hid me for a season, where I didn't have any connection with anyone. I felt lonely and like I was all by myself. It was in that place he wanted me to be still and know that he is God, and that He was perfecting in "ME" everything that which concerns him. If a plant can live under ground for a season, so can you! God has his perfect timing to Reveal who you are in due time! That is your time to finish growing in whom HE has called.

Everyone in the place please stand and as I end, I want you to pair up by two and begin to speak into each other's life. Encourage each other; lift each other up in the Name of Jesus! YOU ARE NECESSARY TO FULFILL GODS PLAN AND PURPOSE IN JESUS NAME!

As the women were pairing up and speaking into each other's lives, Larissa appeared and grabbed Joslyn's hand as she wept and apologized for all that she had done! She explained how she felt like she was losing her brother, but in all actuality, she was gaining a sister, something that she'd never had. Larissa had explained that she had already spoken with the rest of Joslyn's family prior to coming to the conference. She wanted to be sure that when she made it right with Joslyn and subsequently her brother AJ, that she had already taken care of the hardest task of apologizing to everyone else. Joslyn apologized to her as well for anything that she had done to cause the break down in the relationship and in the communication.

Xanthia and her mother walked over and hugged Joslyn and thanked her for everything that's she had done. As Joslyn was talking to Xanthia and her mother Elizabeth, Ramona, April, Darcie, Kim, Darcie's stepmom, Abigail and Ron's wife walked over. It felt like a real family reunion at that moment. Joslyn felt the strength and courage in these women. Each of these women didn't understand what and why their lives were as they were. They wanted clarity! Even though they came to her with their hearts on their shoulders and hopeless, each of them did the work for their lives and now they are becoming the women that they longed to be. They've recognized that they too are Necessary and so worth it!

Joslyn arrived home basking in the events that happened at the conference. She had spent a couple of hours in the parking lot catching up with Xanthia and her mother afterwards, so she arrived home later than expected. When she entered the house through the garage, she could hear the laughter of AJ and Larissa. She knew that God had done his work, yet again!

A New Season

It's Monday, another week had started, and Joslyn didn't want to think about all the messages that she had to return from potential clients. The conference had been more than a month ago and everyone seemed to be doing well. However, now there was a long list of women and men who were waiting for returned calls for an appointment. Roy and Ron had been doing well with honoring their wives and promoting Joslyn's practice just as Elaine had done the year prior. Therefore, in this new season, Joslyn has decided that she needed to expand her practice and accept male clients. Most men find that therapy is not for real men. Roy and Ron are letting men

know that they need someone to talk to as well!

References

King James Bible

New International Version of the bible

The Message Version of the bible

Single, Whole and Holy (Christian Women and

Sexuality) by Joy Jacobs and Deborah Strubel.

About the Author

Jacqueline Russell graduated from Nova Southeastern University where she studied Education and Applied Professional Studies in undergrad, and Curriculum, Instruction, and Technology (CIT) in the graduate program.

Jacqueline is a wife to a wonderful husband and mother of one remarkable daughter and two exceptional stepsons. She is currently teaching elementary school students in Orlando, Florida.

Jacqueline founded "Etiquette on Us Inc." in 2008. The title of the organization means that your behavior is on you. This organization is geared towards empowering young girls to reach their God-Given potential. She teaches these young girls that they must make conscious choices in their lives, and when they do not make conscious choices; their life becomes their own default.

Her favorite pastimes are reading and writing. She also enjoys spending time with her family and friends.

I AM NECESSARY – SO WORTH IT